SEA KAYAKING

JONATHAN HANSON

Outside
BOOKS

W. W. NORTON & COMPANY
NEW YORK • LONDON

For information about permission to reproduce selections from this book, write to
Permissions, W. W. Norton & Company, Inc.
500 Fifth Avenue, New York, NY 10110

The text of this book is composed in Perpetua
with the display set in Monkey
Project Management by Julie Stillman
Composition by Sylvie Vidrine
Manufacturing by Dai Nippon Printing Company
Map Illustrations by Janet Fredericks

Book design by Bill Harvey

Library of Congress Cataloging-in-Publication Data

Hanson, Jonathan.
    Sea kayaking / Jonathan Hanson.
        p. cm. -- (Outside adventure travel)
    "Outside Books."
    Includes bibliographical references (p.) and index.
    1. Sea kayaking. I. Title. II. Series

GV788.5 .H367 2001
797.1'224--dc21

                                        00-048118

        ISBN 0-393-32070-7 (pbk.)

W. W. Norton & Company, Inc., 500 Fifth Avenue, New York, N.Y. 10110
                www.wwnorton.com
W. W. Norton & Company Ltd., 10 Coptic Street, London WC1A 1PU

                1 2 3 4 5 6 7 8 9 0

To Mom,
who said I was crazy,
but always let me go anyway.

ACKNOWLEDGMENTS

My thanks go to good paddling partners: Tommy Thompson, Michael Cox, John Gentile and Katie Iverson, and my wife, Roseann; to paddlers whose exploits far beyond my own have been an inspiration: Karen and Dan Trotter, Jon Turk and Chris Seashore, and Howard Rice; and to paddlers who also happen to be fine editors: John Barstow and Julie Stillman.

CONTENTS

INTRODUCTION

I could, if I wanted to, take a more or less standard approach here and offer you several excellent reasons why you should try experiencing the world from a sea kayak. For example, I could tell you how easy it is to get started: The sea kayak is so beginner-friendly that a complete novice can climb into one and, with 15 minutes of instruction in paddling technique and another 15 minutes practicing safety procedures, comfortably head out for a day trip or even a multi-day tour along a sheltered coast under the eye of an experienced guide. Yet, I could add, that with proper training, experience, and practice, that paddler can undertake self-supported expeditions of a month or more, challenging the most remote coastlines of the world—often in the same kayak he or she started with. There isn't another craft that has that range of capability.

Nor can any match it for the breadth of experience. One of my favorite things to do in a sea kayak is glide noiselessly along the still shore of a lake at daybreak, listening to the cries of loons. Or I might paddle straight out into the Sea of Cortéz on a warm, windless morning, and watch for the spouts of whales or the arcing dorsal fins of a pod of dolphins. But in a different mood I can launch my boat through four-foot surf and dice with the waves surging through an offshore rock garden, or ride the twenty-foot swells of the open Pacific on an exposed crossing to one of the Channel Islands.

Finally, I could tell you, it's all guilt-free. The sea kayak is noiseless. It doesn't pollute the air or water. It creates minimal impact on wildlife. And paddling is splendid, low-stress exercise.

Those are all great arguments to sea kayak—but I'll tell you my secret reason; what it is that, at times, attracts me more than anything else to those slender boats.

Grace.

In a world where giant sport utility vehicles pound the pavement flat, huge jet airliners scream their way through the skies belching fire, and behemoth cruise ships and oil tankers shove their way across the oceans, the simple grace of a sea kayak—the essence of the whole concept we know of as boat distilled to its most elemental form—has the soul-satisfying freshness of a lungful of cool air after a rainstorm. No matter what activities you pursue with your kayak—peaceful contemplation or breathtaking adventure—that grace will follow you, insinuating itself into your actions and your relationship with the boat until you move about on the surface of the sea as though it were your born habitat.

Opposite: West shore of Gabriola Island, south of Johnstone Strait, British Columbia, Canada.
Above: Exploring the Exuma Cays Land and Sea Park, Great Exuma Island, Bahamas.

And you'll find yourself with a new paradigm with which to judge purity of form, function, and movement.

A BRIEF HISTORY OF SEA KAYAKING

Grace has been a feature of the kayak since its beginnings as a hunting craft in the Arctic. No one knows when the first sea kayaks were built, since their materials—driftwood, bone, and ivory frame pieces lashed with sinew, covered with sewn skin hulls—were either recycled into new products, or simply dissolved back into the environment once the boat was abandoned. Some evidence suggests that kayaks were developed over 5,000 years ago. What is certain is the evidence from carvings and illustrations, which show kayaks in use at least a thousand years before the birth of Christ. The apogee of kayak design and use probably came with the Thule Culture, who migrated swiftly across the top of Canada in the 10th century, utilizing both kayaks and larger, open boats called umiaks (the word kayak, incidentally, translates as "hunter's boat," while umiak means "women's boat"). Today's most modern rotomolded plastic sea kayaks would be instantly recognized by those ancient hunters.

The first European explorers were astounded by the speed and maneuverability of the Inuit kayaks, and by the fact that hunters in them often pursued and killed marine mammals weighing thousands of pounds. Nevertheless, the kayak as

graceful tool faded before the technological onslaught of Anglo-Saxon civilization and machinery, and its use shrank to a few isolated villages, a candle flame glimmering feebly just before being extinguished.

But the flame never went out. The skills for building skin-and-frame kayaks continued to be passed on through a few Inuit artisans, and the advantages intrinsic to the craft—lightness, cheapness, agility (and, I'd like to believe, its grace)—continued to be appreciated by a few hunters, so that today it is still possible to find working sea kayaks off the coast of Greenland and in certain other spots, and there are signs that their use might once again be on the rise in this part of the world.

Meanwhile, in 1907 a German tailor named Johann Klepper, adapting several earlier designs, began commercially producing a kayak with a wood frame and a canvas and rubber hull, which could be broken down to fit inside two duffel bags. The boat became popular with tourists traveling by train to seacoasts and lakes, and the seaworthiness of Klepper's design was proved when Captain Franz Romer crossed the Atlantic Ocean in one in 1928 (although he was tragically lost in a hurricane while attempting to complete his voyage from Puerto Rico to the United States). In 1956 Dr. Hannes Lindemann repeated Romer's crossing, with a happier ending. Yet the Klepper and similar folding kayaks remained the obscure

Above: In tropical waters, Fiji, South Pacific. Opposite: Inuit in traditional kayak on Disko Bay, west coast of Greenland.

passion of a few cognoscenti, until a new boat-building material called fiberglass revolutionized the construction of, first, power and sailboats, and then sea kayaks. At last new sea kayak designs—rigid, lightweight, and durable—could be created and produced at low cost. The idea of the sea kayak as a recreational craft began to blossom.

When I began sea kayaking in the early 1980s, it was still very much a nascent sport in the United States, centered mostly in the Pacific Northwest and Atlantic Northeast, with inspiration from Great Britain, which had about a ten-year head start. Since then, the growth—aided by the advent of super-affordable rotomolded plastic kayaks—has been tremendous, with sea kayaks now outselling river kayaks in the United States, and even surpassing canoe sales at the big L.L. Bean store in Maine. In any other sport, such an increase in popularity might have spelled disaster,

raising the specter of overcrowded routes and degraded put-in sites. But we are, after all, talking about the ocean. There's a lot of room out there. While a few popular areas near urban centers have surpassed my idea of optimum carrying capacity, I know a hundred more places where utter solitude is just a few strokes away.

This book will give you a taste of some of those places.

SEA KAYAKING IS INTENDED as inspiration, not as a guidebook, but I've tried to include as much insider advice as possible, to give you a leg up on your research should one or more of these great kayaking destinations draw you to it. Since sea kayakers tend to be an independent lot, I've written each section with the assumption you'll be going on your own. However, there are tour companies listed for nearly all the destinations,

since a guided trip is quite often the most logistically easy way to experience a distant coast.

CHOOSING A TOUR OPERATOR

What should you look for in a tour company? Compared to the venerable world of organized trekking, guided sea kayaking is still in its infancy. But because of the infrastructure already established in other fields, the kayaking business has matured and expanded rapidly. Nevertheless, there remains a huge gap between destinations such as the Pacific Northwest or Maine, where guided kayak trips are a mainstream tourist business, and Madagascar or Tierra del Fuego, where

organized tours have been available for only a few years, and remain the province of one or two companies. Fortunately, in my experience there are very, very few fly-by-night companies to be wary of in the sea kayaking world. Unlike trekking, where anyone can buy a pack and call himself a guide, sea kayaking requires a substantial initial investment in equipment, thus weeding out most scam artists who are out for a quick buck. My overall impression of the current state of the sea kayak touring business is that in popular destinations, competition keeps everyone sharp, and in remote areas you're dealing with people who are there because they love it and enjoy sharing the experience. Either approach works.

The equipment used by tour operators can tell you a lot about them. The best companies use the best equipment, and keep it in good shape. When I led trips, even though it was a tiny, one-man operation, I always provided fiberglass kayaks and top-quality paddles, which I felt enhanced the experience of even a novice paddler. If you can't visit the company, look closely at the photos in their brochure, or ask about their boats and paddles. Good operators will be proud to specify which brands they use. I'd give some slack to small companies operating in really remote regions, however, that might not find it possible to sell off their old gear for shiny new stuff every year.

Another mark of a quality operator is good food. Since sea kayaks can carry a lot of equipment and supplies, the best guides constantly try to outdo each other in the freshness and excellence of their cuisine. Fine meals are almost *de rigueur* on guided sea kayak trips, and most guides (and brochures) are eager to wax eloquent about the fare. Unfortunately, I no longer lead commercial tours, so you've missed out on the most sublime menus of all. . . .

Last, but not least, a good tour company

will involve the indigenous community as much as possible. The best way to do this is by hiring local guides or support crews. The next best way is to support the regional economy by taking the clients to crafts markets or other places where tourist money can be infused on a local level. Making use of local bed-and-breakfasts or lodges is more effective than using chain hotels.

Above all, just talk to the people involved with the touring company you're considering. They should be enthusiastic about their jobs, and excited about visiting the destination, even if they've been there 40 times. There is nothing worse than a tour led by a jaded guide.

Guided tours are probably the best way for novice paddlers to get a taste of sea touring, and they're also great for experienced kayakers who want to experience an area that might be too logistically demanding to attempt otherwise. But the ultimate touring experience has to be a trip you do completely on your own.

THE INDEPENDENT PADDLER

For anyone new to the concept, it's daunting to think of mounting an independent expedition to paddle along a strange coast across the country or around the world—especially to a region where

Opposite: Looking for orcas, Johnstone Strait, off Vancouver Island, British Columbia, Canada.
Above: Sand dunes, Magdalena Bay, Baja, Mexico.

sea kayaking is unfamiliar to the residents. Don't be intimidated. The locals might or might not doubt your sanity, but you'll invariably have the status of celebrity, and thus can almost always get help to accomplish anything from buying food to trucking a hardshell boat 300 miles down a dirt track. With that said, there are a few things you can do to make such trips easier.

Obviously, the most difficult thing to deal with logistically is the kayak. In some areas of the world—the United States and Great Britain, for example—you can rent good-quality, expedition-worthy sea kayaks, but in most Third World regions rentals will either be impossible, or restricted to sit-on-top boats designed for day trips. Since the fit and seaworthiness are vital aspects of a sea kayak, you're generally better off bringing your own.

If you invest in a good folding kayak, such as a Feathercraft or Klepper, you'll rarely be faced with anything more than an excess baggage charge for shipping your boat on an airline. A hardshell boat makes things more difficult and expensive, but by no means impossible. It's vital that you check with several airlines when planning your trip, because policies vary drastically among them, and change so frequently that it's impossible to recommend one carrier over another. One might take your boat as oversize luggage; another might classify it as cargo and insist on shipping it on an entirely different aircraft. Oddly enough, the more remote you get, the less airlines seem perturbed at the idea of carrying a 17-foot-long package. On the world's frontiers, pilots are sanguine about dealing with unusual cargo. (A friend of mine climbed on an ancient jet in Mongolia and found among his fellow passengers a gentleman with two full jerry cans of gasoline, and a woman toting a rifle. The rifle didn't bother him, but the 30 or 40 people puffing cigarettes in the fume-laden cabin did give him pause.)

One downside of kayaking compared to trekking is that, except in a few popular spots, it's nearly impossible to find local guides with their own kayaks, willing to lead a private group on a per diem basis. On the other hand, anywhere there are subsistence fishermen with boats—Mexico, Africa, and South America in particular—you can usually find someone to hire as a consultant and water taxi, or for resupply drops.

The two attitudes that will be your best allies when kayaking in remote locations are patience and flexibility. Third World subsistence economies are in many ways the most functional on the planet. There is always someone who knows someone with a truck or bus to haul equipment, someone with a boat to provide a ferry service, or someone with a guest room or cafe. The trick is to be polite and cheerful, but to just dive in and ask. Believe it or not, having an apparent impediment such as a kayak often leads to more rewarding interaction with the locals than if you arrived all self-contained with a backpack and just disappeared. You'll enjoy your trip more, and the natives will enjoy you more too.

ABOUT THIS BOOK

Since sea kayaking embraces such a vast disparity in skill levels, the book is divided into three parts.

Setting Out introduces trips suitable for beginning kayakers who sign up with a commercial tour, or for independent paddlers with a solid grounding in technique and rescue skills, but not necessarily hundreds of sea miles under their hull.

Deeper Waters features destinations that are a bit more advanced, still possible for novices under the auspices of a competent guide, but requiring more stamina. Independent kayakers should be experienced in rough-water technique, and possess both the skills and equipment (including protective clothing) to survive in more remote areas.

The Outer Limits represents the top level of expedition sea kayaking, truly spectacular areas of the world that will challenge the ability of expert paddlers. The tour operators in these locations—when there are any—generally ask that clients be skilled paddlers on their own before signing up.

Each chapter includes several sections to help you decide if the trip is right for you:

AT A GLANCE

This section is a brief overview of the main characteristics of the trip. It includes Trip Length and Paddling Distance, which give you an idea of how long and how far the trip is.

There are two ratings given for the difficulty of the specific route; one for the physical challenge, the other for the mental challenge. These ratings are numbered 1 through 5, with 1 being the easiest, and 5 the most difficult. You'll note that many, if not most, of these ratings span a range. That's as it must be on the ocean, where conditions can fluctuate drastically—much more so than, say, on a trekking trail.

Physical Challenge. A trip rated 1 signifies a route possible for either a complete novice with a guide, or for an independent paddler with a firm grasp of technique, but not a lot of trip experience. These routes are characterized by sheltered water, short paddling distances (less than 10 miles per day), and protected spots for launching and landing. At the other end of the scale, a trip rated 5 signifies an advanced route that will challenge even expert paddlers. There will be long, open-water crossings, the near-certainty of high winds and seas, and difficult launchings and landings.

Mental Challenge is a bit more difficult to quantify, but in general a 1 rating means the route is near a major population center, so that outside rescue is certain if there is trouble, and there are no factors to create apprehension, such as extremely cold water. A rating of 5 signifies very remote locations where there are significant environmental hazards and little or no hope of outside assistance in an emergency. Even when paddling conditions are benign in such places, the general level of tension is higher.

Prime Time gives the best time of year to visit each region. In some places, such as the Everglades and the Arctic, prime time is really the only time to go, as the off season can be characterized by extremely high temperatures and lots of bugs (Everglades), or the significant logistical problem of an ocean frozen solid (Arctic). In other areas, however, skirting the edges of prime time might be considered in order to avoid crowds, even if the weather might be more unsettled. I've indicated where this tactic might be wise.

Price Range. Two cost estimates are given, the first for an independent trip, the second for an outfitted group trip. For the independent trip I have estimated a range of costs, beginning with a budget trip where you would camp and cook your own food as much as possible, and including the other end of the scale where you might "base camp" in a hotel or resort and paddle out for day trips. Costs for a local kayaking guide are not

included, since in most places such a service simply doesn't exist.

Guided trip costs for sea kayaking tend to vary because of length of the trip and the remoteness of the location, rather than because of the services provided, since the vast majority of guided sea kayak tours include all paddling equipment and food, to reduce logistical and packing problems for the guide. Where this is not the case in this book, the exception is noted.

All trips include an estimate for a night in a hotel at the beginning and end of the trip. All estimates also include land transportation costs from the staging city. Estimates do *not* include transportation to the staging city.

Staging City. The nearest city or town to the launching point where one can expect to be able to resupply with food and other essentials—but not necessarily kayaking gear.

Heads Up. Alerts you to possible trouble spots or hazards.

SUGGESTED ROUTES

This section gives details on the lay of the land (and sea), possible put-ins and landing locations, tides and currents, and points of interest along the way (as well as areas to avoid). You'll note that I've included very little of the "go straight here, turn left there" sort of directions necessary to many destination books. The beauty of sea kayaking is that there are no trails, and very few hard and fast routes. In a sea kayak you are a traveler on a vast two-dimensional plane, and the illusory nature of your path is a blessing that should be exploited as often as possible. When someone asks me how far a paddle it is from Portland, Maine, to Castine, my answer is "It depends." And that's how it should be.

What to Expect

Just what it seems. Here you'll find out the particulars of the area: getting there, weather, sea conditions to be aware of, other environmental hazards, health issues, and so forth. Also included here is general information on accommodations and/or camping.

Guides and Outfitters

A listing of tour companies that offer trips in the area, with contact information and pricing.

Recommended Reading

This section offers suggestions for some guidebooks, and some travelogues or even novels that capture the spirit of the place.

THROUGHOUT THE BOOK you'll find boxes that might cover anything that struck me as quirky or especially interesting, be it flora and fauna or tidbits of history. I've also included four day-trip paddles in unexpected areas, such as New York City and Cape Town, South Africa.

Safety

Many people view sea kayaking as a risky sport. Indeed, in certain conditions and in certain areas, there is an undeniable element of risk in simply being on the water. But far more often the infrequent accidents that happen to sea kayakers are the result of failure of the paddler to do one of two simple things: wear a life jacket, and wear proper clothing. In my instructional books on sea kayaking, I've hit readers hard with their responsibility to wear suitable cloth-ing for the conditions in which they are paddling, and I'll do so here as well. As the axiom goes: To dress to paddle you should dress to swim. Outerwear for kayaking should be designed to prevent or drastically slow immersion hypothermia in the unlikely event of a capsize and subsequent rescue procedure. Where appropriate, I suggest suitable outerwear, but keep in mind that these are suggestions only. There are dozens of variables that determine what is an adequate level of protection for an individual, so consider your own physiology when deciding what to take. One paddler might be perfectly safe wearing a thermal stretch suit in the same conditions where another would need a full dry suit.

Precautions are not necessary to make sea kayaking safe; they are neccessary to *keep* it safe. When I plan expeditions to remote coasts, I do everything possible to avoid testing Yvon Chouinard's premise that "Adventure begins when you screw up."

MY FINAL ADVICE to you is this: Whatever you do, don't assume the trips detailed here are the last great sea kayaking destinations (I hate that term). The freedom granted us by the sea kayak—its ability to probe hidden coves and shallow lagoons—means there are thousands of places left to explore that have been passed up by those in larger boats. Use this book for examples, then go find your own.

Keep safe, be graceful. Happy paddling.

Opposite: Near the head of Marinelli Fjord, Tierra del Fuego, Chile. Overleaf: Sunset, Great Exuma Island, Bahamas.

Johnstone Strait

The dorsal fin of a male orca slides past your kayak,
its tip higher than your head.

An early morning fog had laid a thick, chilly blanket over Johnstone Strait when I left my companions sleeping in their tents and, coffee mug in hand, wandered down to the driftwood-lined shore. I climbed an enormous beached tree trunk out on the point and sat with my legs hanging over the side, directly above where the steep gravel bank plunged into the dark, unrippled water. The silence and stillness were both absolute, and I sat wrapped in peaceful anticipation of the day ahead.

I had finished my contemplations and my coffee, and was just about to head back to camp, when I heard it: a far-off *poosh*, followed by another, and another. I waited, peering into the fog where the silvered surface of the water merged seamlessly with the saturated air, but the silence descended back around me as if no sound had ever been. Wishful thinking? I decided so, and stood to leave, but then something caught my

Early morning encounter with orcas off Kaicash Beach along the west side of Johnstone Strait.

BRITISH COLUMBIA

eye and made me look down.

In the water, down where the dim light from the overcast sky surrendered to the gloom, a barely perceptible ellipse of white moved silently toward me. It ghosted nearer until the white belly also was visible, then, last, the black shape of her back, just a shade blacker than the water itself. Only 20 feet offshore when I spotted her, the female orca was now 15 feet away and still headed toward me. At last, just as I began to fear she must be sick or disoriented, she turned, with her short, curved dorsal fin now cutting the surface, and sideslipped into the gravel, colliding gently and noiselessly.

As I watched, mesmerized, she slowly, luxuriously scratched her belly against the gravel bottom, squirming back and forth in pleasure, arcing tight 180° turns to stay in the thickest accretion of pebbles, raising a slight cloud of silt with each pass. For a full five minutes she scratched while I stood frozen, too wary of breaking the spell to call my friends. Finally, the dome of her head broke the surface and she exhaled a mist of cannery-scented air; then she banked and slid into the depths of the strait.

At another time, in another mood, I might have whooped with glee. Instead I simply smiled and raised my cup in mute but profound gratitude, and climbed off the log. It was the orca who decided to end our encounter with an exclamation point. As I walked up the beach, a small sound, an unfocused *swish*, made me glance behind, to see the orca frozen in midair, a halo of faceted water drops frozen around her. Then she crashed sideways back into the water with a noise that echoed off the forested hill at my back, and elicited a chorus of sleepy voices from the tents: "What was that?" I just smiled and raised my cup again.

THE ORCA, *ORCINUS ORCA*, is the second-largest predator on earth—eclipsed only by the sperm whale—and one of the most intelligent (it is also the second most widely distributed mammal on earth, next to humans). Belying its colloquial name, killer whale, the orca actually belongs to

Overleaf: Coming ashore at Desolation Sound on the Sunshine Coast, British Columbia.

AT A GLANCE

TRIP LENGTH 3 days–2 weeks
PADDLING DISTANCE 5–30 miles
PHYSICAL CHALLENGE (1) 2 3 4 5
MENTAL CHALLENGE (1) 2 3 4 5
PRIME TIME July and August (most orcas, most people), June and September (fewer of both)

PRICE RANGE (INDEPENDENT TRIP) $290–$400
PRICE RANGE (OUTFITTED GROUP TRIP) $445–$1,645
STAGING CITY Victoria, B.C.

Blackfish Sound along the Inside Passage, where the tidal currents can hit 5 knots.

the family Delphinidae, the dolphins.

Although there is only one species of orca, marine mammalogists have identified three distinct types in the area off Vancouver Island, British Columbia: residents, transients, and offshores. Little is known about the offshores. Transients prey on marine mammals such as seals, sea lions, porpoises, and even whales. Residents live in pods of related individuals and feed only on fish, which they find using echolocation (transients rarely echolocate because it would alert their mammalian prey). Residents have a highly advanced social structure, and communicate with each other in a language so evolved that scientists recognize regional dialects.

The Johnstone Strait area, off the northeast coast of Vancouver Island, is home to several of these resident pods, which congregate every summer to prey on salmon. The strait, which averages between 1½ to 2½ miles in width between the Vancouver Island shore and the shores of Hanson and Cracroft Islands, offers sea kayakers the best opportunity in the world to view orcas from close up without disturbing the animals. Since the orcas follow more or less regular routes up and down the strait, groups of

THE MEDUSAE

Johnstone Strait is a good place to spot jellyfish pumping slowly along just beneath the surface, expanding and contracting their almost transparent, umbrella-like bodies in unhurried rhythm. Like all members of the phylum Cnidaria (which includes coral polyps), they have stinging cells, called cnidocytes, lining their tentacles. While not potentially deadly to humans like the dreaded sea wasps of Australia, the Pacific Northwest varieties can cause painful welts if you come in contact with them. So don't do what my friend John did.

In the middle of a crossing between Vancouver and Hanson Island he scooped up a beautiful pale jellyfish in his bailing pitcher to show me, then returned it to the water. A while later he announced that he absolutely had to answer a call of nature, and stroked off a ways to put the pitcher to multiple use. Unfortunately, the jellyfish had left a few of its cnidocytes stuck to the rim, and. . .well, let's just say that John's next couple of days in Johnstone Strait were less than comfortable.

Scanning the sea for dorsal fins, Robson Bight Orca Preserve, between Vancouver and Hanson Islands.

paddlers head offshore on calm days and wait for the sound or sight of them, then position their boats in the apparent path of travel and sit quietly. This allows the orcas to approach or stay away as they please—and typically orcas treat a sea kayak as nothing but a bit of floating debris in their path. I once sat and watched the giant, straight dorsal fin of a male knife through the water straight toward my boat, its tip three feet higher than my head. Just as I began to get nervous, the fin slowly sank until it submerged only feet from my starboard side. I looked down and watched 30 feet of orca pass under me, then the fin smoothly emerged from the water on the other side.

The setting in Johnstone Strait provides a suitable backdrop for these breathtaking encounters. Heavily forested hills, mostly Douglas fir, rise steeply from the water, often shrouded in mist in the early morning—indeed, sometimes all day. Black bears and deer forage along the shore, and bald eagles perch high in the trees. Small fishing boats anchor off the coast during the tightly regulated commercial fishing season, the crews using nets and line to catch salmon. And occasionally a startling apparition churns past: Cruise ships plying the Inside Passage route between Washington and Alaska pass through the strait, to the derogatory remarks of paddlers. (We're told these behemoths pipe closed-circuit views of the passing

scene into the stateroom televisions, so passengers needn't get chilled by going outside.)

Even if there were no orcas here, the Johnstone Strait region would be a lovely destination for its misty Pacific Northwest scenery and abundance of other wildlife. But it's the near certainty of a close encounter with one of the most magnificent predators on earth that defines the Johnstone Strait experience. Whenever I meet another paddler who has kayaked with orcas, our voices adopt the same tone of awe as we speak of it. Wait until you are close enough to a pod of orcas to hear their chirps and squeals through the hull of your boat—you'll know what I mean.

The town of Telegraph Cove.

SUGGESTED ROUTES

Most paddlers drive about 15 miles east of Port McNeill to the tiny, picturesque community of Telegraph Cove (population about 20), with its cottages on stilts over the water, to park and launch. Telegraph Cove is literally around the corner from the best paddling in Johnstone Strait. There are a campground and restaurant there, as well as cabins for rent.

There's really no route *to* Johnstone Strait: Paddle out of the harbor from Telegraph Cove and you're there. You might find orcas 10

minutes after launching.

The best area for spotting orcas is the narrow section of the strait marked by Telegraph Cove on the west and Robson Bight on the east (a distance of about 11 miles), between the Vancouver Island shore and Hanson and West Cracroft Islands.

This is a popular kayaking destination in midsummer (July and August), when the weather is best and orca concentrations at their highest. That's not a problem on the water, where there's enough space for even the worst misanthrope to

Opposite: "Heavily forested hills, mostly Douglas fir, rise steeply from the water, often shrouded in mist."

BALD EAGLES

Very common in the tall fir trees along Johnstone Strait are bald eagles, which, once you learn to watch for them, can be spotted from amazingly far away by looking for the tiny white smudges of their heads (on the adults only; juveniles have dark heads).

Bald eagles are year-round residents of the Pacific coast as far north as the Aleutian Islands of Alaska. Coastal areas allow them to feed on fish during the winter, when many eagles in the interior of the continent

must migrate south. Bald eagles also take advantage of carrion, and will kill birds and small mammals as well when fish are scarce.

Bald eagles build massive nests in the tallest trees (sometimes over 150 feet up), using the same one year after year (a pair often stays together for life). The female usually lays two eggs, which, in the Johnstone Strait area, hatch in May or June.

Checking the chart at dusk.

find solitude. Camping sites on the strait, however, can be scarce, because of steep banks and thick undergrowth. If you're with a private group, it helps to keep your numbers down to six or fewer members, so you can exploit smaller sites. Also, you'll have better luck away from the more heavily traveled Vancouver Island shore. Cross to Hanson or West Cracroft Islands, or head up through Blackfish Sound (watch the tidal currents through here, which can hit 5 knots). Once you find a good spot, it's best to base there and do day trips, rather than attempting to find a new site each night. Keep in mind that as you get farther

from Johnstone Strait proper you reduce your chances of orca encounters, although by no means do you eliminate them.

WHAT TO EXPECT

The large (population 325,000) yet beautiful city of Victoria, on the southern tip of Vancouver Island, is a major ferry terminus from the city of Vancouver, on the Canadian mainland and from Washington State. Victoria, with its lovely gardens and buildings, is a relaxing stopover before or after a paddling tour. Accommodations range from superb Victorian hotels to backpacker hostels. North of Victoria is Nanaimo, another ferry terminus and home to a couple of sea kayaking shops. Scheduling and fare information for BC Ferries is available by calling (250) 386-3431. Washington State Ferries is at (206) 464-6400.

From Victoria or Nanaimo, Highway 19 travels all the way up the east coast of the island. It's about 270 miles to Port McNeill (population 3,000) the nearest town of note to Johnstone Strait. Port McNeill has grocery stores and hotels.

One way to avoid the summer rush is to visit the strait at the edges of the season, in early summer or September. The weather will be more unsettled then, and orca populations lower—but you'll have a better chance of camping right on the strait. A sure way to avoid campsite worries is to travel with an organized tour. The major tour groups stake out comfortable, semipermanent camps each season (the legal and moral issues of which are hotly debated among independent paddlers).

Although Johnstone Strait is protected from the weather and seas of the open Pacific, storms or wind can make the strait dangerous for paddlers—especially if you go during the edge of the season. Fortunately, given its narrowness, it's difficult to get caught out by a storm *unless* you're not paying attention. Take a radio with a weather band and stay abreast of developing conditions. Even in summer the air temperature can be cold, and rainstorms might last for a few minutes or a few days. If you go on your own, take a truly waterproof tent of a size that won't cramp you. A separate dining fly is a nice option so you don't have to sit inside during every shower.

Water temperatures are always cold here—50°F or below in the summer. Ignore the paddlers you'll see dressed only in shorts and t-shirts when it's sunny (generally with their life jackets bungeed on the rear deck as well), and dress for immersion. A Farmer John wet suit is a good choice, or at the very least a full suit of thermal stretch fabric. The latter is more comfortable during the fine, warm days that bless the strait in July and August.

The cruise ships that pass through the strait could run down a sea kayaker without so much as a thump, and the captain would never see you. Although hours often pass with no traffic at all, you should always use caution when crossing the strait. Since the big ships stick to the middle of the channel, the best way to cross is to paddle offshore a half mile or so, then look to make sure no ships are in sight before crossing the middle.

The 40- and 50-foot whalewatching boats operating in the strait are used to watching for kayakers, but you should *never* assume they've seen you, and never expect to be given right of way. These boats are often encountered much farther inshore than the big ships, and since they are looking for orcas as well, your chances of crossing paths with them are greater.

Although it would be very difficult for someone in a sea kayak to seriously harass an orca, be considerate in your encounters. Never, ever attempt to chase them; let them come toward you instead. Some guides recommend tapping on the deck of the kayak if an orca is coming close, just to help it pinpoint your location. No orca in Johnstone Strait has ever so much as bumped a kayak, much less attacked one.

One big advantage of a trip in Johnstone Strait is that it's not far from Seattle, Washington, the source of about 99.9 percent of all the sea kayaking gear in the universe. It won't matter what you've forgotten at home; you can replace or rent it there or at the Ecomarine store in Vancouver.

GUIDES AND OUTFITTERS

Several excellent companies lead fully outfitted tours into Johnstone Strait. Most tours are suitable for beginning paddlers.

Northern Lights Expeditions has two decades of experience in Johnstone Strait. The company offers six-day trips that include all paddling gear, tents, and meals; you must bring your own sleeping bag. Ecosummer Expeditions also has a long history here.

NORTHERN LIGHTS EXPEDITIONS
P.O. Box 4289
Bellingham, WA 98227
800-754-7402
www.seakayaking.com
$1,195 for 6 days

ECOSUMMER EXPEDITIONS
P.O. Box 1765
Clearwater, B.C.
Canada V0E 1N0
800-465-8884
www.ecosummer.com
$445 (3 days)–$1,645 (2 weeks)

RECOMMENDED READING

■ *ADVENTURING IN BRITISH COLUMBIA*, Isabel Nanton and Mary Simpson (1996. $16.00. Sierra Club Books.) Oriented toward outdoor activities.
■ *HILL GUIDES—VICTORIA AND VANCOUVER ISLAND*, Kathleen Hill and Gerald Hill (1998. $15.95. Globe Pequot Press.) Contains more detailed information on Vancouver Island.

The Everglades

*A world where water and land are woven together
like a tapestry.*

A river fifty miles wide and six inches deep creates the most unusual ecosystem in North America.

When the heavy rains of summer overfill the enormous reservoir of Lake Okeechobee, the water fans out in a vast sheet that flows down an imperceptible slope of ancient limestone bedrock toward Florida Bay, the protected patch of Caribbean sandwiched between the tip of the mainland and the Florida Keys. Continuously awash, immense plains of a bladed sedge called saw grass give the "uplands" of the Everglades an uncanny resemblance to a Nebraska prairie, punctuated by occasional limestone swells called hammocks, on which grow trees such as royal palm, gumbo-limbo, mahogany, and strangler fig.

Eventually the broad river reaches the ocean, but the interface is so obscure as to defy attempts to point out where mainland ends and islands begin, or where fresh water turns

". . .a warp and weft of habitats—saw grass, dense tree stands, mangrove swamps, fresh and salt water."

FLORIDA

GULF OF MEXICO

ATLANTIC

Lake
Okeechobee

Everglades

Ten Thousand
Islands

Everglades City •   Miami •

*Everglades
National Park*

Flamingo •

*Florida
Bay*

to salt. As the runoff cuts its way into the peaty soil overlying the porous oolite limestone, serpentine channels appear, intersecting and looping in infinite labyrinths, gradually broadening until a last turn reveals a narrow glimpse of nothing but blue water on the horizon. But take another detour and you could lose the sea for hours.

In spite of the overwhelmingly flat landscape, the Everglades mixes an astonishingly diverse warp and weft of habitats—saw grass, dense tree stands, mangrove swamps, fresh and salt water—which in turn suppport an equally diverse profusion of fauna. Over 300 species of land and sea birds can be found here: Anhingas fly underwater spearing fish; great white egrets stand in silent ambush in the shallows, and ospreys dive-bomb from the air. Rare roseate spoonbills are sometimes seen at the southern tip of the mainland. A locally endangered raptor, the snail kite, feeds almost exclusively on a single species of snail. Mammals, too, find dozens of niches to fill, and range from terrestrial species such as armadillos, opossums, deer, and bobcats, to those that forage the water's edge, such as raccoons and otters, to purely aquatic species such as dolphins

and manatees. Among reptiles, the crocodiles and alligators obviously reign as the top predators, but less dramatic examples such as terrapins and rat snakes are common. Loggerhead sea turtles lay their eggs on the beaches of Cape Sable each summer.

Everglades National Park encompasses nearly one and a half million acres. But it's the tangled labyrinth of islands and channels along the coast that attracts canoeists and sea kayakers, especially the 100-mile-long Wilderness Waterway, which meanders between Everglades City in the northwest and Flamingo in the southeast. The route is an excellent one, since it takes in most of the Everglades' habitats as well as stretches of both fresh and salt water. Along the way, the Park Service has erected nearly 50 campsites, ranging from simple beach clearings to sturdy wood platforms on stilts, called chickees, with outhouse facilities.

Fortunately for misanthropic paddlers like myself, you're not restricted to the Wilderness Waterway (which, incidentally, is also open to powerboats). There are literally thousands of possible routes among the channels and islands. And for independent exploration, sea kayakers have a definite advantage over canoeists, since we can

---

AT A GLANCE

TRIP LENGTH ½ day–7 days	PRICE RANGE (INDEPENDENT TRIP) $320–$475
PADDLING DISTANCE 5–100 miles	PRICE RANGE (OUTFITTED GROUP TRIP)
PHYSICAL CHALLENGE ① 2 3 4 5	$50–$945
MENTAL CHALLENGE ① 2 3 4 5	STAGING CITY Miami, Florida
PRIME TIME Mid-December–mid-April	HEADS UP Alligators

MANGROVES

The red mangrove (*Rhizophora mangle*) common to the outer islands of the Everglades, is the most salt-tolerant of the several species of mangroves in south-

l white
her up
tent of
ken up
through
pearing

al fash-
ertilized

seeds actually germinate on the plant and sprout a short root before dropping into the water. The seedling floats with the current until the root contacts a muddy bottom, then takes hold. Borne on equatorial currents, mangrove seedlings have occasionally crossed the Atlantic Ocean.

The millions of dead leaves that fall from mangroves to the muddy sea floor are colonized by bacteria and fungi, which begin to break them down so the fragments can be consumed by larger detritivores, which in turn have been shown to be preyed upon by over 100 species of fish.

Gulf of
.
e you a
islands
tropical
stiltlike
ile mud
ugh seas
cies and
any oth-
and mil-
ranches.
ients for
ks in the
ile skirt-
, as hun-
into the
roaches.
to your
ading up
y: Broad
eral oth-

ers. It's like being dropped into the Congo. High branches of mahogany trees sprout bromeliads, epiphytic plants that derive their nourishment from rainwater and air. The water under the boat is black and mysterious, even blacker under floating mats of vegetation and where it's shaded by overhanging figs and palms. And here and there, if the light is just right, you'll spot the loglike three-lump shape of an alligator—nose, head, and back—as it waits for a passing meal. Park officials emphatically warn against swimming in the channels.

Alligators don't make their presence known in the Everglades solely by eating things. During the dry season they excavate deep holes into the substrate under ponds, which helps keep them filled with water, thus supporting many other species. Local guides, never loathe to trade on the fearsome reputation of the region's signature species, like to point out these excavations: "Ooh, take a look at that 'gator hole. Betcha there's a big one down there."

hore, you'll learn how vital mangroves are to the health of tropical coastlines.
s National Park.

Exploring this world of water, it's difficult to remember that the biggest threat to the health of the Everglades is the lack of water. Since early in the 20th century, massive canals and ditches have been siphoning off the water flowing into the region, diverting it for agriculture and a burgeoning urban population. The influx of new residents to the Miami area alone requires adding 200,000 gallons of water every day. The resulting lowering of the water table has been serious enough to account for a 90 percent decrease in the number of breeding birds within the park. Once you have completed your journey through the channels and islands, it will be hard to avoid some sense of responsibility to help save this unique area. Several major pieces of legislation have been proposed to put teeth into existing conservation plans. Perhaps a few calls to legislators from indignant paddlers will help convince the congress to act.

Since 1947, when Marjorie Stoneman Douglas wrote her inspirational book *The Everglades: River of Grass*, and the national park was created by President Truman, public awareness of the Everglades has grown from a perception of it as worthless swamp to a realization of its astounding beauty and diversity. But a good 40 years before that, two explorers of the Everglades, Edwin Dix and John McGonigle, gave us a good reason to visit—and protect—this place, when

ALLIGATORS AND CROCODILES

Southern Florida is the only area in the world where crocodiles (genus *Crocodylus*) and alligators (genus *Alligator*) coexist. The order Crocodylia, to which both belong, represents animals already roaming the earth before *Tyrannosaurus rex* evolved. They have survived for 160 million years, including the extinction of the dinosaurs, with their antedeluvian appearance almost unchanged. Male American alligators can reach lengths of 14 feet or so; American crocodiles grow to about 12 feet. They eat nearly anything they can catch, from crabs and fish to raccoons and birds (and, in some areas, the odd neighborhood dog).

Belying this fearsome reputation, however, alligators and crocodiles are among the very few reptiles that evidence parental care. The females of both species guard the large mounds of soil and leaves in which they bury a clutch of several dozen eggs. When the young hatch in July or August, they emit a series of squeaks, which signals the female to unearth them and escort or even carry them to water. Once the hatchlings enter the water, however, they're on their own.

The American alligator, once endangered, has

made a remarkable recovery and is now quite common in the southeastern United States. The American crocodile has not been so fortunate, its numbers estimated at no more than a few hundred and its future uncertain. Incidentally, a third member of the crocodilians is occasionally seen in the wilds of Florida: the spectacled caiman, a South American species that was imported by the thousands for the junk pet trade. Many were released or lost in the Everglades when their owners tired of them or the caimans grew too big (what *did* those parents think would happen when they brought them home for Christmas?).

Sunset, Ten Thousand Islands, Everglades National Park. The Wilderness Waterway begins here.

they wrote: "It is rather a good thing to have a little of wonderland left."

SUGGESTED ROUTES

The Wilderness Waterway is an excellent introduction to the Everglades for its variety and secure camping sites. You can cover it in either direction, from Everglades City in the northwest or Flamingo in the southeast. From Everglades City, the route samples the Ten Thousand Islands region, skirting sections of open coast, then begins probing inland up slow river channels, crosses Oyster Bay, Whitewater Bay, and little Coot Bay before exiting the Buttonwood Canal to Flamingo. The route is well marked, and explained in the visitor's guide.

If you'd like a more impromptu journey, take a right instead of a left when you paddle out of Everglades City and you'll be in the Ten Thousand Islands chain. It's less traveled than the waterway, and easier to get away from powerboats. Even here, however, the Park Service maintains scattered campsites; the visitor's center can tell you where camping is allowed. But you're free to land anywhere to explore.

Besides the 100-mile-long Wilderness Waterway, there are several short canoe trails in the park. You could experience a sampling of the Everglades' habitat without camping, by taking advantage of these short trails, which range from 5 to 10 miles in length. A full

Along the Wilderness Waterway the Park Service has erected campsites, from simple beach clearings to platforms on stilts.

resource is *A Canoeing and Kayaking Guide to the Streams of Florida* (see Recommended Reading).

WHAT TO EXPECT

The Everglades are undergoing a major transition right now. In 1992 Hurricane Andrew flattened thousands of acres of mangroves, as well as other tree species of the interior and hammocks. The results are still obvious, with many dead trees and others—especially the tenacious mangroves— knocked over but still alive. To our human-sized frame of reference for time, such events seem like disasters—but it's important to remember that mangroves evolved with regular hurricane cycles, and so will regrow and recolonize. The debris doesn't detract from the scenery or the experi-

ence; it's simply a lesson in progress in long-term environmental fluctuation.

Miami is just a few miles outside the east entrance to Everglades National Park, and you can find anything you need there, up to and including paddling gear. There is only one hotel inside the park boundaries, the Flamingo Lodge in Flamingo. It's plain but has a certain charm, and is within smelling distance of the mangroves.

You need a permit for overnight stays in the park at any time of year. They are available from the visitor's center, and must be obtained within 24 hours of your departure (no advance permits).

Although air and sea temperatures are generally mild during winter, remember that the Ten Thousand Islands are subject to weather from the open Gulf of Mexico. Always monitor weather channels, and check with the Gulf Coast Visitor's Center in the park for current conditions and warnings.

There are venomous snakes in the Everglades, including coral snakes, water moccasins, and rattlesnakes. However, bites are extremely rare, and if you watch where you put your hands and feet it's unlikely you'll run into trouble. Of more concern is the Portuguese man-o-war, a stinging jellyfish. While not deadly, a brush with the nematocysts of one of these is extremely painful. Watch for the blue bubble-like shape of individuals stranded on beaches.

Clothing for paddling the Everglades should be lightweight and offer full sun protection. A wide-brimmed hat is a must—but not too wide-brimmed, or it can blow off.

GUIDES AND OUTFITTERS

Loon Bay Outfitters offers half-day introductory tours of the Everglades. Nantahala Outdoor offers an all-inclusive tour of the Wilderness Waterway.

LOON BAY OUTFITTERS

941-417-2264
www.florida-everglades.com/loonbay
$50 for half-day tour

NANTAHALA OUTDOOR CENTER

13077 Highway 19 West
Bryson City, NC 28713
888-662-1662 ext. 333
www.nocweb.com
$945 for 7 days

RECOMMENDED READING

■ *A CANOEING AND KAYAKING GUIDE TO THE STREAMS OF FLORIDA*, Lou Glaros and Doug Sphar (1988. $13.95. Menasha Ridge Press.)
■ *THE EVERGLADES: RIVER OF GRASS*, Marjorie Stoneman Douglas (50th anniversary edition, 1997. $18.95. Pineapple Press.)

Anhinga drying wings, Anhinga Trail, Everglades National Park.

Exuma Islands

Warning: Paddling here can be hazardous to your work ethic.

The Gulf Stream, an ocean current so mighty that it moves more water—roughly 25 million tons *per second*—than all the rivers of the world combined, surges northward through the Florida Straits east of Miami at a constant 4 knots (almost 5 miles per hour). So many vectors of force—flow rate, wind speed, Coriolis effect—combine here that sea level at the west edge of the current is some two to three feet higher than at the east edge, as if the stream were careening around some gargantuan banked racetrack.

In the late 17th century, when Spain's empire was at its mightiest, hundreds of Spanish ships, many of them loaded with fabulous amounts of treasure—including gold, silver, and jewels—used the straits as a slingshot to carry them north into prevailing westerly winds for the trip back across the Atlantic. This steady stream of loot was an irresistible lure for one of

Beach campsite, Exuma Cays Land and Sea Park.

EXUMA ISLANDS

the most famous groups of criminals in history: the English pirates, who operated with the open, and often gleeful, approval of the Crown.

The Spanish ships used every trick they could think of to outwit, outmaneuver, and out-run the privateers' raiding ships, but in the end one fact always worked against them: They were loaded to the gun-nels with cargo, and the pirate ships weren't. Furthermore, the pirates had the most tactical-ly perfect base imaginable from which to stage their lightning-quick raids, and into which they could disappear at will when pursued: a group of islands known as the Bahamas.

The advantages of the Bahamas as a raiding base are obvious. First, there are a whole lot of them to hide behind: 700 islands and another 2,000 smaller cays. The shifting shallows of the Grand Bahama Bank grounded many armed Spanish warships sent to rout the pirates, who knew the waters intimately. And the pirates could exploit the same current as their victims when it was time to head back to England and trade in their booty.

But I, for one, refuse to think that it was all coldly objective reasoning on the part of the pirates. For could any but the dullest among them have failed to notice that, in between raids, they got to hang out in one of the most beautiful areas in the world? It was the quintessential paradise: palm-thatched islands, gen-tle surf creaming on perfect white sand beaches, clear, warm water, and lots of sun. No wonder piracy attained such a romantic image.

The sanguinary days of the Bahamas are long past, but time hasn't dimmed their attrac-tion. Those scenes of sea, surf, and sand make for the sort of vacation poster that stops pedestrians in their tracks as they pass by the travel agency, bundled up in layers against a December sleet storm. The Bahamas have attained an almost iconic status as a place to *relax*, to shrug off the cares of the world for a week or two.

The overwhelming majority of visitors to the Bahamas head for one of the resorts that pep-per nearly all the larger islands and cays. But the typical resort scene, which might seem like heav-en to a confirmed urbanite, holds little attraction for most sea kayakers. For us there is a corner of

---

AT A GLANCE

TRIP LENGTH 7–14 days	PRICE RANGE (INDEPENDENT TRIP) $750–$1,800
PADDLING DISTANCE 45–100 miles	PRICE RANGE (OUTFITTED GROUP TRIP)
PHYSICAL CHALLENGE ①② 3 4 5	$1,500–$2,100
MENTAL CHALLENGE ① 2 3 4 5	STAGING CITY George Town, Great Exuma Island
PRIME TIME December–May	

the Bahamas that still basks in an unhurried, uncrowded atmosphere: the Exuma Islands.

The Exumas (ex*oo*mas) comprise a 100-mile-long chain of 365 islands and cays, mostly uninhabited, about 40 miles southeast of Nassau. At the southern end of the chain are two large islands, Great Exuma and Little Exuma, with an area greater than the rest of the islands combined. Here is where most of the residents live and where most resort development is concentrated. Spanning 20 miles in the middle of the chain is the Exuma

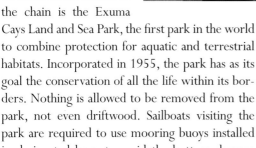

Cays Land and Sea Park, the first park in the world to combine protection for aquatic and terrestrial habitats. Incorporated in 1955, the park has as its goal the conservation of all the life within its borders. Nothing is allowed to be removed from the park, not even driftwood. Sailboats visiting the park are required to use mooring buoys installed in designated bays, to avoid the bottom damage caused by repeated anchorings. And get this: per-

sonal watercraft are forbidden within the park boundaries. Whoever suggested that should be beatified.

The southeast-to-northwest line of the Exumas perches on the edge of a vast, shallow shelf called the Grand Bahamas Bank. The water on the west side of the islands averages about 40 feet deep for thousands of square miles—a play-ground for divers. To the east is Exuma Sound, a modest name for a dra-matic feature: From the 40-foot-deep shelf, the bottom of the ocean sud-denly plunges away straight down to depths of thousands of feet, an effect that can produce verti-go in passengers of low-flying planes.

The cays themselves are a paddler's dream. White sand beaches are in abundance here, sloping gradually into gentle surf. Palm trees shade the beach, and silver buttonwood trees cluster around ponds in the interiors of larger cays. Many man-grove estuaries serve as nurseries for crabs, fish,

Above and opposite: Guide Steve Johnson paddles his Klepper folding kayak along the shore in the Exuma Cays Land and Sea Park, the first park in the world to combine protection for aquatic and terrestrial habitats.

THE BIRD THAT DANCES FOR DINNER

In shallow tidal flats and mangrove estuaries in the Bahamas you might spot a handsome wading bird called a reddish egret. A lovely gray overall, with soft reddish highlights, especially around its head, the red-dish egret has a fascinating hunting strategy. Instead of waiting motionless in the shallows for small fish to swim close, like most herons and egrets do, the red-dish egret performs a dance: It holds its wings out and

bounds slowly from side to side through the water. The motion startles small fish that might otherwise escape detection by remaining motionless them-selves. When they dart for cover, the egret stabs with its long, slender bill to snag them.

Reddish egrets were decimated in the 19th cen-tury for their plumes, which were used to adorn ladies' hats. Fortunately they have made a comeback.

Breaking camp and preparing to set out. Large water bottles are about to be stowed in the kayaks' hatches; fresh water is very scarce in the Exumas, so ample supplies must be carried.

and birds. And of course the reefs offshore provide superb snorkeling. Huge formations of elkhorn, brain, and star coral are common.

Not all exploration in the Exumas involves natural phenomena. On a couple of cays are the remains of failed resort ventures, which have been converted into odd little wayfarers' stops by visitors. In one falling-down ruin is an impromptu library where you can take or leave a book; on another cay is a bizarre, rambling driftwood-and-flotsam folk sculpture created by successive additions.

Now I'm going to suggest something slightly different from the usual how-to-go advice: If you decide to visit the Exumas, don't go on your own; sign up with a guided trip.

Oh, it's not that you couldn't do it all yourself. There are no particular dangers here, and the paddling certainly isn't hazardous. It's just that the Exumas, as with the Bahamas in general, are antithetical to every permutation of work ethic you might have, and it's fun to be able to indulge while someone else does the chores. Dinner cooks—you snorkel. Lunch dishes need washing—you're napping. Route planning? Just tell me which way to paddle.

On a couple of cays the remains of failed resort ventures have been converted into wayfarers' stops.

The single problem with this approach is if your work ethic repertoire includes feelings of guilt when someone else is doing it all. But that's easy to counter, as you watch from the shade of a palm tree while your guides scrub the pots and slice paw-paws for dessert. Just remember one thing—they get to stay here after you go back to the sleet storm.

SUGGESTED ROUTES

If you insist on *working*, and want to explore the Exumas on your own, there are two options. The first, and most comfortable, is to arrange a base camp and do day trips from there. A base "camp,"

in this case, could be as straightforward as one of the many resorts in George Town on Great Exuma, or, better, one of the dozens of private vacation cottages available by the week, located on the big islands and several of the cays. Don't be fooled by the seemingly small land area on some of these private cays; you can easily spend a week exploring the coast and reefs of even the smallest, with time out for frequent snorkeling stops.

If you want to tour the Exuma Cays Land and Sea Park, the best base is on Staniel Cay, about 10 miles from Conch Cut, the southern border of the park. The park comprises a chain of cays spaced almost ideally for easy paddling. The

Above: Assembling a folding kayak, and (top) sailing in one.

too; that is, they don't stick out much on the horizon, and on a couple of crossings in the Exumas, especially with surface haze on the ocean, you might find yourself out of sight of your goal for the day. Bring a large-scale chart and a compass, and plot your course carefully, even if it seems like an easy jump to the next island.

Most commercial tours of the park begin in Staniel Cay and end in Norman's Cay, a total distance of about 45 miles. It's a good itinerary for an independent trip as well, easily covered in a week or so. A complete tour of the Exumas, beginning in George Town and ending in Norman's Cay, can be accomplished in two to three weeks.

WHAT TO EXPECT

Either Nassau or George Town serves as a base for exploring the Exumas. Neither has a dearth of places to stay and eat; all tend to be fairly expensive during peak season, with discounts offered during summer.

You'll never have trouble finding a hotel or resort anywhere in the Bahamas. George Town is no exception. At the Club Peace and Plenty, all the rooms have balconies overlooking the harbor, and the restaurant is above average as well. But if you really want to live it up, and for less than you might think, there are also houses available on a few privately owned cays, where you can indulge in the complete Gilligan's Island fantasy. One such spot I found is on a 450-acre cay; the house (3 bedrooms) rents for $1,500 per week—not bad at all if you divided it up among three couples (the millionaire and his wife, the professor and Mary Ann. . .).

Staniel Cay is accessible by charter flight from Nassau or George Town (a passenger/mail boat also goes there from George Town). There are private cottages for rent on Staniel, as well as hotels. The yacht club also has a couple of cottages for rent. Staniel Cay is famous as the underwater setting for the James Bond film *Thunderball*.

longest crossing is about 4 miles; most are much shorter. The park ranger station is on Waderick Wells Cay, about one-third of the way up the chain. The biggest cays in the park, from south to north, are Bell's, Hall's Pond, Waderick Wells, Cistern, Hawksbill, and Shroud. There are dozens of smaller cays, most with their own reefs.

The park itself is a little over 20 miles long, ending just south of Norman's Cay, which gained infamy in the 1980s as the hangout of the drug lord Carlos Lehder, before he was captured and jailed in the United States Norman's Cay is now more, er, low-key, with its own beachfront villas for rent. Don't miss the half-sunk C-46 airplane in the harbor, courtesy of an inept drug pilot.

While distances might be short, the cays are

THE LIZARD THAT BEGS FOR BREAKFAST

If you're not prepared, you could be excused for fleeing in panic after landing on Allen's Cay, at the far northern edge of Exuma Cays Land and Sea Park, when several three-foot-long lizards come running toward you. These are Allen's Cay Iguanas (*Cyclura cychlura inornata*), a subspecies found nowhere else. But all the iguanas are doing is expecting to be fed, since many yachties and paddlers have taken to feeding them lettuce and fruit.

Despite their apparent abundance, these iguanas are endangered, since they live on only two tiny islets of Allen's Cay (only a few are present on the third).

Charter flights also land on Norman's Cay, so you can arrange a dropoff on one island and the pickup on another.

Fresh water is scarce in the Exumas—one reason the islands have been spared much development. You should carry all you need with you. While it's sometimes possible to beg water from sailboats, it would be both foolish and rude to count on doing so as your main supply. You can usually ask for water at the bigger resorts.

December through April is high season in the Bahamas. The rains normally begin in May and last through November; hurricane season is June through November, with December as a possibility. Pushing either edge of the season will reduce your encounters with other tourists. Prevailing winds in winter are from the northeast, but frequently shift around the compass.

Not surprisingly, given the islands' position on the edge of the Gulf Stream, currents can be strong there. A good sailing guide is the best book you can buy for detailed information about currents and other local concerns.

GUIDES AND OUTFITTERS

Piragis Expeditions, offers eight-day tours of Exuma Cays Land and Sea Park, from Nassau. Ecosummer Expeditions runs nine-day tours of the park, and 15-day tours of the Exumas. For air charters try Clear Air, Nassau (242–377–0341).

PIRAGIS EXPEDITIONS

105 N. Central Ave.
Ely, MN 55731
800-223-6565
www.piragis.com
$1,500 for 8 days all-inclusive

ECOSUMMER EXPEDITIONS

P.O. Box 1765
Clearwater, BC, C0E 1N0 Canada
800-465-8884
www.bcadventures.com/ecosummer
$1,500 for 9 days
$2,100 for 15 days

RECOMMENDED READING

■ *THE EXUMA GUIDE: A CRUISING GUIDE TO THE EXUMA CAYS,* Stephen Pavlidis (1997. $29.95. Seaworthy Publications.) Although written for sailors, this book is also perfect for kayakers. Includes practicalities plus history, natural history.

■ *FODOR'S BAHAMAS* (2000. $15.95. Fodor's Travel Publications.) The most up-to-date guide to the Bahamas, although short on detail for the Exumas.

Caribbean Coral Reefs

*Rain forests, jaguars, and barrier reefs,
two hours from Texas or Florida.*

It's not been proven statistically, but the sea around Belize's barrier reef probably causes more boats to capsize than any other sea kayaking area in North America.

It's a constant threat, and can strike capriciously any member of a group. You might be paddling comfortably in calm, windless conditions, with the 78°F water barely rippling as you hover over a shallow patchwork of turquoise-tinted sand and coral outcrops. Then it just happens—in the blink of an eye you're upside down. You don't even set up for an Eskimo roll, because the crystalline water with its flashing schools of tropical fish sucks you out of the cockpit like an irresistible force. You pop to the surface next to your capsized kayak, while your companions look on with a notable lack of concern.

"*Darn*. Fell in *again*. Oh well, while we're here we might as well do some snorkeling."

The Belizean recipe for a paddling paradise is

Coming ashore along the barrier reef off Lime (low) Cay, coast of Belize.

YUCATAN
PENINSULA
CARIBBEAN

difficult to fault: warm, clear water, palm-shaded islets of white sand, the second-longest barrier reef in the world, plus three of the four significant coral atolls found in the Caribbean Sea. And if you wish, you can enter a completely different world and paddle up broad, slow rivers under a tropical forest canopy, with howler monkeys screaming and toucans croaking overhead, and jaguars and ocelots slipping through the undergrowth. All within a two-hour flight from Houston or Miami.

Belize's barrier reef (which, incidentally, is also the second-largest biological formation on earth) guards the country's entire coast in a great, sweeping, 185-mile-long arc. The reef ranges in distance offshore from 10 miles in the north to 40 in the south. Belize's territorial waters actually exceed its land in area. Over 200 small islands, called *cays* (pronounced "keys") delineate the reef in a long, ragged chain. Many cays are tiny, impenetrable clusters of red and black mangrove, permanently awash, vital for their role as nurs-

Ambergris Cay
Belize City
Half Moon Cay
Dangriga
Glover's Reef
BELIZE
Punta Gorda
Gulf of Honduras
GUATEMALA

eries for birds, fish, and marine invertebrates. Others are larger, with fringing beaches of blindingly white sand surrounding low shrubs and tall palm and coco plum trees, like a proverbial South Seas castaway isle. The astonishing variety of life on and around the cays—220 species of reef fish, for example—led the United Nations to declare Belize's barrier reef a World Heritage Site, recognizing that its loss or degradation would result in "a harmful impoverishment of the heritage of all nations of the world."

Between the mainland coast and the reef the ocean is shallow, but east of it, toward the open Caribbean, the bottom drops rapidly. Out of these cobalt depths rise Belize's three coral atolls, ring-shaped groups of islets surrounding enormous, shallow lagoons. The water around the atolls is as clear as air, and many species not found closer to shore breed here. It's a divers' and snorkelers'

Overleaf: Calm water, Glover's Reef Atoll, Southwest Cay.

AT A GLANCE

TRIP LENGTH 7–10 days, though it's completely worthwhile to escape for 4 or 5 days
PADDLING DISTANCE 30–65 miles
PHYSICAL CHALLENGE ① ② ③ 4 5
MENTAL CHALLENGE ① ② 3 4 5
PRIME TIME December–March (cool and relatively dry), April and May (hotter, more insects, but fewer people)

PRICE RANGE (INDEPENDENT TRIP) $280–$750
PRICE RANGE (OUTFITTED GROUP TRIP) $990–$1,695
STAGING CITY Belize City, Belize

heaven. On the outside of some of the atolls you can be paddling along 20 feet above a flat coral bed, then with a vertigo-inducing jolt glide over an edge that drops hundreds of feet. In addition to thousands of fish such as damselfish and butterfly fish, the magnificent underlying coral beds of the lagoons are ornamented with tube sponges, anemones, and fan and black coral. Birders can spot magnificent frigate birds with eight-foot wingspans. Island fauna includes, astonishingly, lizards, boa constrictors, and raccoons, the descendants of colonizing individuals washed off the mainland on logs.

All this marine beauty has not been ignored by tour operators. Most tourism in Belize is oriented toward scuba enthusiasts, and most of the development is in the northern cays. The largest cay, Ambergris, boasts a good-sized town, San Pedro (population 2,000), with numerous hotels, restaurants, gift shops, and bars. Eight miles south of Ambergris Cay is Cay Caulker, and a smaller town. These two cays are the hubs for the majority of visitors to the reef. Small-boat commercial fishing formerly provided the majority of income, but tourism has leapt far ahead in this part of the country. (Interestingly, many former commercial fishermen have become sportfishing guides, specializing in fly-fishing expeditions for such elite species as bonefish and permit.)

Belize is an experiment in progress for the concept of ecotourism as a conservation tool. To a greater degree than any other Central American country, Belize seems determined to preserve its natural beauty, both on land and sea—and it is blessed with a good foundation from which to do so. Unlike most neighboring countries, Belize has never suffered the catastrophic environmental and social consequences of a civil war. Over 60 percent of the country's forests remain relatively intact (compared to a tragic 2 percent in El Salvador). The government has designated preserves, national parks, and other protected areas that cover nearly one-third of the land area—a greater percentage than any other country in the world. In addition, offshore preserves and parks encompass over 100 square miles, including Half Moon Cay and Blue Hole Natural Monuments. Independent from Britain since 1981, Belize boasts a stable parliamentary democracy and remains a member of the British Commonwealth (which, charmingly, means Queen Elizabeth is still the nominal head of state). The literacy rate is an impressive 91 percent.

All of which doesn't mean that there aren't threats to this apparent naturalists' dream world—threats that only reinforce the role of responsible ecotourism as a building block of both preservation and a healthy economy.

Belize must import most of its food, oil, and manufactured goods. Such a situation leaves a country at the whim of international economies and trade deficiencies, and fuels the push for

Fishermen (and their sons) go door-to-door with their daily catch in the southern town of Punta Gorda.

Sergeant's Cay, barrier reef off Belize, a fine example of a coral atoll (see below).

CORAL ATOLLS

Charles Darwin was the first scientist to correctly surmise how coral atolls are formed, a conclusion he reached using nothing more than keen observation and superb deductive reasoning. His theories of fringing, barrier, and atoll reef formation survive to this day with little alteration.

Corals are tiny relatives of anemones, exhibiting the same radial symmetry and prey-capturing tentacles. Hermatypic, or reef-forming, coral polyps build bases of calcium, and succeeding generations of polyps build upon the dead bases of their ancestors. Coral reefs are massive aggregations of living and dead coral that grow in the sunlit waters along some coasts and around certain volcanic islands, the latter known as a fringing reef. Often, over hundreds of thousands of years, the summit of the island erodes or simply sinks beneath the surface of the ocean. The result is a shallow lagoon surrounded by a coral reef, usually with several small islands emerging from the sea—a coral atoll.

Top: Evening on Glover's Reef Atoll, a 25-mile paddle from Dangriga on the mainland.
Above: A short hop to an islet on a calm day.

banana farmers are lobbying heavily for changes in the status of preserves to allow large-scale agriculture, which would require complete razing of the forest. Belize's huge national debt is further temptation to grab quick profits at the expense of long-term environmental health. Fortunately, tourism is now dicing with agriculture as the leading industry; it is hoped that this will encourage the government to continue its preservationist policies.

Tourism, of course, brings its own dangers and abuses. Aside from the basic problems of habitat loss when resorts are built in fragile environments, there are losses through careless behavior, from divers who denude reefs of black coral and lobster, to pleasure boaters whose thoughtlessly tossed anchors demolish the reef structure itself. Belize's challenge is to balance access with protection—and that is where low-impact activities such as sea kayaking can play a vital role. How's that for an environmentally conscious reason to visit paradise?

SUGGESTED ROUTES

Although you can kayak directly out of the resort cays of Caulker or Ambergris (there are marine reserves at both the north and south ends of Ambergris Cay), most sea kayakers will want to either avoid completely or at least get away from the bustle of the northern cays. To do so you can head south or east.

The dozens of cays directly south of Caulker (Chapel, Hick's, Long, Montego, and others) support a series of smaller resorts and lodges, some luxurious, some primitive, some no more than campgrounds or cabins, mostly depending on the size of the cay. Any of them is suitable as a base for sea kayaking, either for day trips or as a hub for longer excursions. You could paddle directly from Belize City to these cays, as no crossing is longer than 3 or 4 miles.

Farther south, development thins out even more as the cays arc away from the mainland

industrialization and resource exploitation within the country. Belize still battles deforestation: Lumber is always a highly marketable commodity, and commercial sugar, citrus, and

The Snake Cays are relatively solitary, yet only a short paddle from the southern town of Punta Gorda.

(and from Belize City, the largest town on the coast). The southern cays are where experienced kayakers looking for more isolation will head. If you are skilled enough to be comfortable with open-water crossings, you can tour nearly the entire barrier reef south from Caulker, camping on small islands such as Bluefield Range, Colson Cay, Half Moon Cay, and Northeast Cay. Gentle white beaches make for easy landings on most of these cays, and an abundance of reef fish ensures fresh seafood for anglers.

The most spectacular, and most logistically challenging, destinations for paddlers visiting Belize are the atolls far offshore. Since they lie not only quite a distance from the mainland, but beyond the protection of the barrier reef, they are

Top: Male magnificent frigate bird. Middle: Hotel Turtle Inn, Placencia Village. Above: Colorful signs along Placencia's 15-mile sandy beach show the coastal Creole village's laid-back attitude.

usually reached by charter boat. However, a group of strong kayakers with open water experience can paddle east from the coastal town of Dangriga, making a 10-mile hop to tiny Tobacco Cay and its cluster of modest resort cabins, and then a 15-mile jump to the Glover's Reef Atoll, which is now a marine reserve. There is accommodation on Glover's Reef at Glover's Atoll Resort, which has both cabins and camping sites. The total round-trip mileage for an expedition such as this would be over 60 miles.

A very accessible alternative for those who don't wish to venture as far offshore lies within a few miles of the southern coast, northeast of the town of Punta Gorda, which is literally the end of the road in Belize. The Snake Cays are not part of the barrier reef, but consist their own sort of mini-reef of hundreds of islets, developed from a submerged limestone ledge at the mouth of a large bay. Most of the islets are impenetrable mangrove scrub, but others are larger, sandy, and shaded with palms, coco plum, and sea grape. The Snake Cays are relatively unvisited, yet can be reached from Punta Gorda without the need for a chartered boat. On one of the islands, Wild Cane Cay, archaeologists have found remnants of a Mayan coastal trading center. A round-trip through the Snake Cays from Punta Gorda covers roughly 30–40 miles.

WHAT TO EXPECT

Leave the wet suit at home; bring the sunscreen and insect repellent. With water temperature averaging 78 to 84°F, there's very little danger of hypothermia. If you're camping on your own, a screen tent will help keep mosquitoes and sand flies at bay.

The official language of Belize is English, so you'll have no trouble communicating. Belize City, the largest city and main airline terminus, has developed a somewhat rough reputation for aggressive panhandlers and the odd mugging. While the reputation is not

MANATEES

Although they look like a cross between a seal and a whale, manatees are neither—they belong to the marine mammal order Sirenia, a group including dugongs and sea cows. All are gentle, slow, and herbivorous, with front flippers and paddlelike tails. The West Indian manatee is found in shallow waters off the coast of Belize, where its population seems to be at least holding its own (manatees in other areas have been drastically reduced by hunting and collisions with powerboat propellers).

Sea kayakers often catch glimpses of manatees, though rarely for long due to their shyness. Many local guides in Belize offer manatee-watching trips in small boats, often including snorkeling. The Belize government has strict regulations about how close observers may come to the animals.

unjustified, if you stick to the main tourist areas and keep out of shady areas after dark, you'll have no more trouble than in any similar-sized American town. If you're with a tour, of course, your guides can be expected to shepherd you in the right direction. The people of Belize, by and large, have retained their Caribbean friendliness, rather than adopting colonial reserve.

Accommodations in Belize City range from hostels with shared baths up to the *very* nice—and expensive—Radisson Villa Wing.

You'll have no trouble stocking food in Belize City or other towns, but bring your own paddling gear. The few kayak rentals that are available are sit-on-tops made for snorkeling excursions.

GUIDES AND OUTFITTERS

Several companies offer excellent guided tours of the cays and atolls. Island Expeditions runs trips of varying duration along the barrier reef. Slickrock Adventures runs tours of Glover's Reef Atoll, and has a base on one of the islands there.

ISLAND EXPEDITIONS

368-916 West Broadway
Vancouver, B.C. V5Z 1K7 Canada
800-667-1630
www.belizekayaking.com/trips
$990 for 6 days

SLICKROCK ADVENTURES

P.O. Box 1400
Moab, UT 84532
800-390-5715
$1,695 for 10 days.

RECOMMENDED READING

■ *BELIZE, ADVENTURES IN NATURE,* Richard Mahler and Steele Wotkyns (1997. $18.95. John Muir Publications.) Good travel information oriented toward natural history.
■ *CENTRAL AMERICA, THE ROUGH GUIDE,* Peter Eltringham et al (1999. $19.95. The Rough Guides.) Very good inside information for independent travelers.

The Cyclades Islands & Crete

Paddling through the cradle of human civilization and myth.

Are the storied Ionian and Aegean Seas that wash the shores of Greece really such a deeper, more midnight-toned shade of sapphire than other seas? Does the sun really burn with a more brilliant, golden light on the spare Grecian hillsides? Or is it an illusion, an optical effect created by contrast among the bold strokes of primary colors that make up the landscape: whitewashed buildings rising in ranks from the shore, red-tiled roofs, the dense green shade of tamarisk and juniper trees. Perhaps it's not the light or color itself, but the heady awareness of human history that heightens perception and frames each day spent in Greece as in no other country except, perhaps, Egypt.

No matter—the source of the illusion is not as important as its effect, which is to amplify every experience, to lend more import to landmarks and passing scenes, and to make even a short passage in a small boat seem like an epic

The town of Fira on Santorini perches atop the caldera's edge overlooking the Sea of Crete.

CYCLADES
ISLANDS

DELOS
To Athens
MYKONOS
PAROS
NAXOS
IOS
SANTORINI

SEA OF CRETE

Iraklion

Hora Sfakion   CRETE

journey of discovery—almost, well, Homerian, if you would.

Beginning long before the heroic but hapless Odysseus "weathered many bitter nights and days in his deep heart at sea, while he fought only to save his life, to bring his shipmates home," the ocean has exerted a constant, profound influence on life in Greece. A full one-fifth of the country's land area is islands—1,400 of them—which ring the mainland from the Ionian Islands (Odysseus's home) off the west coast, to the largest, Crete, in the south, to the Sporades and Aegean Islands in the northeast, many of which are much closer to Turkey than to the Greek mainland.

The history of Greece is, at its heart, the history of humans, and that extends to its islands, which have been inhabited for thousands of years. In fact, two of Europe's earliest Bronze Age civilizations, the Cycladic and the Minoan, were born on Greek islands, the Cyclades and Crete, respectively. Beginning nearly 5,000 years ago, the people of the Cyclades, a group of islands just off the southeast coast of the mainland, began producing exquisite, slender marble statuary—forerunners of the great classical Greek marble works,

but more abstract in form—and also developed an extensive maritime trading economy, a tradition that has continued right up through 20th-century celebrity Greek shipping tycoons whose freighters cover the earth.

The enigmatic Minoans blossomed a bit later (and superceded the Cycladic culture), but made up for it with metalwork and ceramics of astonishing beauty, in addition to the luminous frescoes discovered on Crete by the English archaeologist Sir Arthur Evans in the early 1900s. Much about this sophisticated civilization is still unknown, even what they called themselves: Evans named them the Minoans after King Minos of Greek mythology.

The artifacts of the Cyclades and the Minoans, and other, later civilizations, including those of the famous city-states, still remain on the Greek Islands. Visiting the sites of their palaces and temples, and studying their sculptures and paintings in regional museums, provokes powerful emotions: These are, after all, the very foundations of our own civilization.

And then there's a happy coincidence. The sea kayaking in Greece is splendid.

Start with 300 days of sunshine a year. Mix

AT A GLANCE

TRIP LENGTH 7–10 days
PADDLING DISTANCE 20–25 miles
PHYSICAL CHALLENGE ① 2 3 4 5
MENTAL CHALLENGE ① 2 3 4 5
PRIME TIME April–May, September–October

PRICE RANGE (INDEPENDENT TRIP) $750–$1,400
PRICE RANGE (OUTFITTED GROUP TRIP)
$1,800–$1,950
STAGING CITY Athens, Greece

with warm Mediterranean water. Add beaches that can be of the purest crushed-shell white or a striking volcanic black. Top it off with an efficient ferry system that lets you hop between islands at will, and an equally efficient network of hotels, pensions, and hostels. Did I mention superb food? The result is a perfect stage for an archaeo-kayaking expedition.

As with many other paddling destinations in urbanized Europe, Grecian sea kayaking is best done on the day-trip plan, with stays in hotels or, better, small pensions each night. The spare Greek landscape, while it provides a handsome backdrop to the coast and its ports, has little to tempt wilderness paddlers (and the Greeks have a distinctly laissez-faire attitude toward litter, spoiling many otherwise pleasantly deserted spots).

The 30 or so major islands of the Cyclades (pronounced kick*lah*des) are a natural destination for those who like to mix coastal paddling with open crossings. If the weather and time permit, you can hop between any adjoining islands in a half-day. Otherwise, the ferry system serves as a built-in sag-wagon. The small, central island of Delos is one of the most important archaeological sites in Greece, and the mythical birthplace of Apollo and Artemis. Farther south is the astounding Santorini, formerly a large round island, now a much smaller, ring-shaped one, thanks to a massive volcanic eruption in about 1650 B.C., which destroyed the existing Minoan towns and, many believe, gave rise to the story of Atlantis.

Crete, at 175 miles in length a much larger island than all the Cyclades put together, is its

own world. The north coast is where most of the large towns (and oversized tourist hotels) are; the south coast is more precipitous, and the villages smaller, and that is where the best paddling is.

Still, you'll need to spend at least a few days in the north in the capital, Iraklios, for its spectacular archaeological museum and the nearby reconstructed palace complex at Knossos, the center of Minoan civilization.

Whether you explore the Cyclades or Crete—or, if you have time, both—you'll spend sun-drenched mornings on the water, afternoons retracing the rise of western culture, and evenings in waterfront cafes over meals of grilled seafood, topped off with potent shots of ouzo, with lively bouzouki music in the background. If poor Odysseus had had it so easy, he wouldn't have minded taking 20 years to return home.

SUGGESTED ROUTES

It would be possible to undertake a sea kayak voyage in Greece and camp the entire route; there are enough deserted beaches and uninhabited islands to make such a strategy feasible. However, to be frank, there would be little point in doing so unless your budget demanded it. Greece is a country almost completely molded by humans and their history, not just in the towns and historic sites but in the countryside as well. To try to fashion a sea kayak trip there into any semblance of a wilderness journey would be missing the point. You'll get more out of your stay by immersing yourself in the culture.

The astonishingly complex Greek ferry system allows a paddler with a hardshell kayak to

Above: Repairing nets, Mykonos, Cyclades Islands. Opposite: Sunset along the southern coast of Crete.

Golden late-afternoon sunlight at Tramonto on the island of Mykonos.

begin in Athens (Piraeus, actually, but it's right next door) and hop from island to island at will. Thus the choice of routes is limited only by your imagination, budget, and schedule. If you plan your trip for the spring or fall, before or after the peak tourist season, you'll have no trouble finding lodging in hotels or pensions each night, obviating the need for reservations and schedules.

If you have time, a tour of both the Cyclades Islands and Crete is worthwhile because of the varying landscape and the contrast in the ancient civilizations found in each region.

CYCLADES ISLANDS

In addition to their rich history, the Cyclades Islands make an ideal starting point because of their proximity to Athens and the international airport. In fact, a group of strong paddlers could dispense with the ferry system altogether and paddle directly to the archipelago, since no hop is longer than 10 miles. However, the ship traffic is heavy and constant in these channels, so unless you are strong—and alert—you're better off hitching a ride. I suggest beginning in Santorini (also called Thira) and paddling along the precipitous inside walls of the caldera (the sunken core of the eruption), an awe-inspiring experience. The main town of Santorini, Thira, perches dramatically on the top of the caldera's bluff. Accommodation there—especially with a view—is expensive, but worth it. Other islands in the Cyclades worth visiting include Paros, Naxos, Ios, Ikaria, and of course the archaeological site of Delos, where overnight stays are forbidden.

CRETE

On Crete, an easy tour of the southern coast, and the one most used by the very scarce com-

mercial kayak tour groups, starts at Agia Galini, beneath the mountains just west of Cape Lithino, and proceeds west, stopping in small villages at night, and winding up in Hora Sfakion, a tiny port wedged between mountains and sea. West of Hora Sfakion the coast becomes progressively more precipitous. If you have a folding kayak, you can take advantage of the bus system that connects port towns on the southern coast. Car rentals are also available.

The southern coast of Crete is generally a windward shore, making for stress-free paddling, but occasionally contrary patterns can come up. Fortunately landing sites are never out of sprinting distance. Tidal currents are not a problem.

WHAT TO EXPECT

Not only are Greeks friendly to strangers (more so as you get away from tourist centers and high season); they're also likely to ask all sorts of personal questions that would be considered taboo during a first conversation in the United States. Don't be offended; just smile and tell them how much you make a year, how old you are, how much your spouse weighs. . . .

If you are invited into someone's home for a drink or meal, even someone of obviously low income, don't try to pay them. A small memento or gift is better, especially if given to one of the children.

The Greek tourism industry—hotels, pensions, and restaurants—takes its vacation in winter: Most establishments close down completely. The best times to go are April and October. You might find restricted hours at some businesses, but in general you'll have an easy time finding places to stay and eat, at prices significantly lower than summer rates.

Most of the islands function well as full-service communities. You'll have no trouble

Dining options in Crete: A tavern on Venetian Harbor in Hania on the northwest coast (top), or a seaside campsite along the south coast (above).

buying groceries if you don't want to eat out all the time. Don't plan on replacing broken or lost paddling gear, however, even on Crete or other large islands.

You'll find warm water and lots of sun. Dress accordingly, in long-sleeved, lightweight shirts of nylon or a similar quick-drying material. I like the sturdy Ultimate Hat for headgear: It's wide enough to shade ears and neck, but not so wide as to flop over your eyes in a wind.

GUIDES AND OUTFITTERS

The Nantahala Outdoor Center runs trips along the southern coast of Crete including an all-inclusive eight-day inn-to-inn tour from Iraklion. Active Journeys offers a seven-day tour of Crete. Piragis Northwoods Company runs trips to the Ionian Islands on the west coast of Greece from Athens.

NANTAHALA OUTDOOR CENTER
13077 Highway 19 West
Bryson City, NC 28713
888-662-1662 ex. 333
www.nocweb.com
$1,950–$2,150 for 8 days

A LANDSCAPE CREATED BY HUMANS

In the 9,000 years since early neolithic times, when humans first began to alter their habitat in a conscious and permanent fashion, the landscape of Greece has experienced a profound transformation. The rocky hillsides visible from the sea today, although beautiful in an ascetic way with their sparse cover of shrubs and small trees, bear no resemblance to the forested land of thousands of years past. The transformation began early, with massive land clearing to make way for olive trees beginning as early as the 6th century B.C., when Solon of Athens urged landowners to plant them, and in fact made cutting one down a capital offense (olive trees were so important to the economy of early Greece that the Grecians considered the tree a direct gift to them from the gods). Olive tree roots, however, are poor at binding soil, so erosion followed. Centuries of grazing by goats and the cutting of native trees for firewood and lumber further reduced the original forest to scattered fragments in the north of the country. The result is that the habitat of Greece today is just as much the product of humans as are the columns of the Parthenon.

Approaching Hora Sfakion, a tiny port wedged between mountains and sea on the southwest coast of Crete.

ACTIVE JOURNEYS

4891 Dundas St. West #4
Toronto, Ontario, Canada M9A 1B2
800-597-5594
www.activejourneys.com
$1,800 for 7 days

PIRAGIS NORTHWOODS COMPANY

105 N. Central Ave.
Ely, MN 55731
800-223-6565
www.piragis.com
$1,900 for 7 days

RECOMMENDED READING

■ *THE GREEK ISLANDS, THE ROUGH GUIDE,* Mark Ellingham et al (1998. $17.95. The Rough Guides.) Good general touring guide to the islands.

■ *THE HILL OF KRONOS,* Peter Levi (1981. Elsevier-Dutton Publishing. Out of print.) A charming introduction to Greece and the Greek people.

New York City

uh? is the reaction of most people when you mention paddling in New York City. Yet not only is the New York City area fascinating to explore with a kayak, the city parks department even has designated kayak launch sites in the boroughs and Manhattan that can be used by anyone who purchases an inexpensive permit. And although it's a decisively urban setting, there's some world-class birding here as well.

For a sea kayaker used to wilderness destinations, the New York area takes some adjustment. There are some familiar ocean hazards to beware of, such as tidal currents, which can exceed four knots in the East River (which isn't a river but a strait, and also boasts some impressive

whirlpools), and the essentially open-ocean conditions of the Lower Bay—but most hazards around New York are of the man-made variety. Wakes from even slow-moving large ships can catch a distracted paddler unaware, but the real danger is from the boats themselves, especially the ferries which seem to be everywhere. As a kayaker you are not only at the bottom of the food chain, but are essentially invisible to the pilot of any large ship. Also, despite hundreds of miles of shoreline, in many areas there are very few actual beaches for launching and landing, which is why the well-spaced parks department sites are valuable.

There are dozens of paddling routes around

the area, including the 30-mile circumnavigation of Manhattan itself, But the best introduction to Big Apple kayaking is in the enormous, island-filled Jamaica Bay, adjacent to JFK Airport. The wildlife refuge in Jamaica Bay is a vital stopover for migrating birds of over 300 species. The west section of the bay, a better destination than the stagnant east section, has excellent access from several points in Brooklyn, such as Canarsie Park or Brooklyn Marine Park.

Paddling distance can be anywhere from 2 to 5 miles, depending on your route.

Clockwise from upper left: in a ship graveyard, Arthur Kill area of New York harbor; near the Staten Island Ferry; off the Statue of Liberty.

Masoala Peninsula

*Exploring the eighth continent—
a biological wonderland.*

I magine a full-grown chameleon that can curl up on a penny, or a mouse-sized lemur, the smallest primate in the world. Imagine a primitive mammal that can provide two dozen of its offspring with milk—at the same time. Imagine the Lost World of Sir Arthur Conan Doyle come to life, its animals and plants molded through splendid isolation into a thousand unique forms.

Born of the African landmass 130 million years ago, Madagascar now breaks the Indian Ocean swells in solitude 250 miles east of Mozambique. With an area of 230,000 square miles—slightly smaller than Texas—it is technically "just" an island, albeit the fourth largest in the world. But size has nothing to do with why biologists have tagged this particular island with the lofty title of the Eighth Continent. In the hundred thousand millennia since its geologic

Dugout meets kayak along a jungle waterway, Masoala Peninsula, Madagascar's northeast coast.

MOZAMBIQUE

MADAGASCAR

Mozambique Channel

Masoala Peninsula

Maroantsetra •

Antananarivo

INDIAN OCEAN

umbilical cord was cut, Madagascar's Cretaceous African ecosystem has reveled in its independence and isolation, evolving and radiating to produce one of the most unique assemblages of life on the planet.

Consider that over 80 percent of Madagascar's plants—and 90 percent of its trees—are endemic; that is, they are found nowhere else in the world. Nine out of ten of the island's reptiles are also endemic, as are fully half the birds—the latter being especially noteworthy since birds are highly mobile and normally widespread. Mammals? Madagascar is the only home for two families of primates, the lemurs and indrids (lemurlike animals with an eerie howl), plus a third that has only one member, the remarkable aye-aye, which uses an elongated finger to probe for larvae and insects inside dead logs in the northern forests. Among the other insects of the island are the world's largest and smallest butterflies.

Its unequaled diversity guarantees that visitors to Madagascar, no matter how well traveled they might be, will be overwhelmed by new sights and experiences.

On a map, the northern tip of Madagascar looks like an enormous, crested bird looking east into the Indian Ocean. The hooked beak of the bird, some 60 miles long, is the Masoala Peninsula, home to one of the densest stands of rain forest on the island.

On Masoala, the smooth, white sand beach, only feet wide in places, exists in a delicate state of neutrality. It courts immersion on one side by the sapphire waters of the Indian Ocean, the full force of which is held back by a bulwark of coral reefs backing shallow lagoons. On the other side, the rain forest strains to plant its tentacle-like roots just an inch or two farther toward the sea, to shade another centimeter of sand under its broad-leafed canopy. Palm trees fighting for sunlight often overhang the surf.

That narrow zone happens to be just wide enough to beach a sea kayak and pitch a tent.

Sea kayakers in Madagascar act like children caught between two favorite rides at Disneyland. The forest exerts a powerful atavistic pull, sweetened by a significant dearth of large hazards (there are no venomous snakes in Madagascar, nor large cats). Every leaf is a potential new universe, with

---

AT A GLANCE

TRIP LENGTH 8–13 days	PRICE RANGE (INDEPENDENT TRIP)
PADDLING DISTANCE 60–120 miles	Not recommended
PHYSICAL CHALLENGE 1 ② 3 4 5	PRICE RANGE (OUTFITTED GROUP TRIP)
MENTAL CHALLENGE ① 2 3 4 5	$1,100–$1,550
PRIME TIME October–December	STAGING CITY Antananarivo, Madagascar

Early morning on Nosy Mangabe, a little island and nature preserve off the west coast of the Masoala Peninsula.

chameleons, frogs, and spiders perfectly con-
cealed in folds and crevices. Harmless ground and
tree boas poise utterly motionless, and lemurs of
a dozen sorts rustle in the canopy.

On the other hand, there is the turquoise sea
and its corals, butterfly fish, parrot fish, and
Moorish idols. The water is almost preternaturally
clear inside the reef, so you can practically hang in
one spot and watch the parade. Fisherman casting
from shore or boat can occasionally snatch a
bonito for a fresh seafood dinner, or you can bar-
gain with local dugout pilots for crayfish.

In the end, though, it's usually the forest that wins by a lemur's whisker. There's just so much to see that you become jealous of every moment not spent peering up tree trunks or under logs. Try to relax on the beach—no go. You might be missing something. And that's as it should be here: After all, you can rest when you go back to work.

Many sea kayaking destinations make you feel as though you've stepped back in time. Madagascar makes you feel like you've been transported to a past epoch—you almost expect a vast herbivorous dinosaur to rear its head over the forest canopy and gaze at you, chewing. There are no giant lizards here, but 100 million years of isolation has preserved a world every bit as fascinating as it must have been when Cretaceous seas first broke the island free of Africa.

Charles Darwin didn't stop in Madagascar during his voyage on the *Beagle*; the ship passed by just to the south. One wonders what the effect on his thinking would have been if he had experienced this evolutionary laboratory so soon after the comparatively modest sampling he puzzled over in the Galapagos. Perhaps *Origin of Species* would have appeared 20 years sooner (but then, perhaps the world wouldn't have been ready yet anyway). What is certain is that Madagascar was recognized as a biologist's heaven long before Darwin missed it. The French explorer Philippe de Commerson, after a visit in 1771, wrote:

"May I announce to you that Madagascar is the naturalist's promised land? Nature seems to

Above: The rain forest shades a narrow strip of smooth, white sand beach on Tampolo Point.

WILL IT BE LOST?

Parts of Madagascar could pass for Eden, but, like the biblical parallel, this Eden could be lost soon if current trends don't change.

Madagascar is a poor country—the sixth poorest in the world—and its growing population still relies on subsistence farming and harvesting to live. Unfortunately, this has contributed, along with commercial logging and clearing for coffee plantations during colonial rule, to the loss of four-fifths of the island's original forest cover. What grows in its place, in the absence of cultivated fields of rice and cassava, are hardy, but nonnutritious, African grasses resistant to fire. Worse, erosion frequently takes over and sends topsoil by the ton down flooding rivers, to be lost to the sea. The forest trees, which evolved with few competitors, are unable to reclaim abandoned land with any speed.

With little other foreign investment likely in the near future, Madagascar has much to gain from a sensitively run ecotourism industry. Such operations can infuse money into local communities, provide sustainable, high-quality jobs for residents, and promote conservation of the resources that attract tourists. Caution must be employed, of course, so that the industry doesn't metastasize and destroy what it seeks to promote, but the potential for good is extremely high.

Storm approaching, Nosy Bihento, off Masoala Peninsula. Cloudbursts bring welcome cooling.

have retreated there into a private sanctuary, where she could work on different models from any she has used elsewhere. There you meet the most bizarre and marvelous forms at every step."

SUGGESTED ROUTES

Most commercial sea kayak trips to the Masoala Peninsula begin in the small town of Maroantsetra, at the head of Antongila Bay formed by the peninsula. There is air service to Maroantsetra from Antananarivo, although in the dry season the town can also be reached by a very rough, 350-mile drive up the coast. There are a couple of small hotels here. Most of the other boats you'll see here will be dugout canoes, still used as working craft by Malagasy fishermen.

From Maroantsetra, the route simply heads south along the forested west coast of the peninsula toward its southern end. Along the way is the little island of Nosy Mangabe, a nature reserve used as a base by pirates in the 18th century, now protected as a home for the aye-aye, among several hundred other species. Twelve hundred acres in extent, Nosy Mangabe rises to a forested summit over 1,000 feet high. This one island alone is worth several days of exploration.

The coast of the peninsula toward its tip is mostly sand, making for easy landings, with stretches of rock to provide variety and perches for birds such as pygmy kingfishers and egrets.

The fringing reef at the southern end of the Masoala Peninsula (*Cap Masoala*) creates sheltered paddling and shark-free snorkeling, with several good camping sites within reach (watch for pretty little red-clawed crabs in the undergrowth). The commercial tours stop at the Masoala Peninsula for several days of poking around on land and sea, before returning north. You can also venture up the Ambanizana River, where you'll think you've been dropped into a Tarzan movie. Sometimes a powerboat is used as a backup on this trip for when the wind makes paddling impossible, and to ferry the group back to Maroantsetra.

WHAT TO EXPECT

The people of Madagascar are as diverse as the flora and fauna. Many appear to be of direct African descent; others more closely resemble Malaysians (the first humans to reach Madagascar, 1,500 years ago, arrived from Indonesia). All are proud to be *Malgashes* (don't refer to them as African), although there are 18 official tribes, delineated more on the basis of ancient kingdoms than ethnicity. Malagasy people tend toward a quiet politeness to outsiders, but curiosity soon takes over if you persevere at conversation. A high birth rate combined with a short life expectancy has resulted in a youthful population: Over half are under 20.

While it would be possible to mount an independent sea kayaking expedition to Madagascar, I wouldn't do so myself—yet. The concept of ecotourism is still in its infancy on the island, and little infrastructure exists to help solo travelers deal with logistics. Even the experienced tour companies that lead groups here stress in their pre-trip packets that itineraries and schedules are extremely flexible, and subject to road conditions, rainfall, local guide availability, and a host of other mercurial factors. Letting a professional guide handle such exigencies removes the stress from the trip. Since even organized tours in Madagascar are subject to many impromptu changes of plan, you'll never feel like you're on a theme park ride.

If you do decide to brave it on your own, I strongly recommend taking a folding kayak, which will make it far easier to hire transportation on the island. From the capital of Antananarivo you can arrange transport to the port town of Maroantsetra on the east coast, close to the Masoala Peninsula. One advantage to an independent traveler is the strong subsistence economy of Madagascar, where almost everyone knows someone who can arrange

THE TRAVELER'S TREE

You're likely to see the traveler's tree (*Ravenala madagascariensis*) before you get into the rain forests of Madagascar: Its image is on the country's seal and the logo of Air Madagascar. A relative of the banana tree, the traveler's tree is so called because of the store of fresh water to be found hidden in the hollow bases of its leaf stems.

Looking like a giant fan, the ravenala has a skinny, palmlike trunk topped by a spray of large leaves arranged in a single plane; it is 30 to 60 feet tall overall. The bases of the leaves form catchments that hold pure water, and a passerby with a long, sharp stick can puncture the leaf and release up to a quart.

As a further confirmation of the wonderful oddity of Madagascan evolution, the traveler's tree can be pollinated by lemurs, which feed on nectar in the tree's flowers and become dusted with pollen in the process.

Top: Sunrise on Nosy Bihento. Above: The people are diverse, some of African descent, others of Malaysian origin. Most speak French.

the surface, which do no good to the skins of folding kayaks. Also, even in the sandy stretches of beach, black boulders can rear their heads just beneath the surf.

Parts of Madagascar receive over eight feet of rain a year, which means that even during the dry season showers are a regular occurrence. Bring a good tent, and an additional tarp to serve as an awning so you won't have to hole up during every cloudburst. Fortunately the rain is usually a welcome cooling-off.

Madagascar is in the malaria belt, so you'll have to take prophylactic medicine. The Centers for Disease Control (CDC) in the United States recommend Larium, which is effective but has numerous side effects. Consult your doctor, and if he or she is not familiar with malaria drugs try to find one who is. The best way to avoid contracting malaria is—as much as possible—to avoid getting bitten. Wear long sleeves and pants, and take a tent with mosquito netting if it is not provided by the outfitter. Mosquitoes are most active around dusk; use repellent and mosquito coils as well.

GUIDES AND OUTFITTERS

Kayak Africa runs a couple of trips to the Masoala Peninsula that include airfare from Johannesburg, South Africa. They use Klepper folding double kayaks. Coastal Kayak Trails also operates on the Masoala Peninsula; their fully inclusive trips vary in length and can be customized to suit.

KAYAK AFRICA
1 Salford Rd.
Mowbray, Cape Town, South Africa 7700
27-21-689-8123
www.kayakafrica.co.za
$1,200 for 8 days; $1,650 for 13 days

COASTAL KAYAK TRAILS
P.O. Box 50238
Waterfront, Cape Town, South Africa 8002
27-021-439-1134
www.kayak.co.za

almost anything. Although a few residents speak English, you'll do much better with a working knowledge of French, still an official language.

Water temperatures close to shore in Madagascar are warm, but long sleeves are a good idea, for both sun and mosquito protection.

Paddling conditions inside the reefs tend to be benign, but watch for strong easterly and southeasterly winds, especially in the afternoon. Also watch for coral heads lurking just beneath

A narrow double-ended boat with outriggers and lateen sail has been the sailing vessel of choice on the Indian Ocean for thousands of years. Its simplicity makes it easy to build and reliable.

RECOMMENDED READING

■ *IN SEARCH OF LEMURS,* Joyce Ann Powzyk (1998. $17.95. National Geographic.) Wonderful narrative of a scientist's work in Madagascar.

■ *THE EIGHTH CONTINENT: LIFE, DEATH, AND DISCOVERY IN THE LOST WORLD OF MADAGASCAR.* Peter Tyson, et al (2000. $27.50. Avon Books.) Insightful look at both people and nature in Madagascar.

Lake Malawi

A freshwater sea in the heart of Africa.

Waiting to launch a dugout, Lake Malawi. While the water is fresh, the lake should be treated like an ocean.

Take a deep breath for the next sentence. A limnologist will answer your first, astonished question about Lake Malawi, blurted out as soon as you look over the side of your kayak into the water, by informing you that it is an ultraligotrophic reservoir, permanently stratified with a warm epilimnion overlaying a colder hypolimnion.

Um, okay. What the heck was the question? What you asked was how any lake could be so utterly pure and transparent that tiny, brilliantly colored tropical fish flitting among rocks 15 feet beneath the surface seem close enough to grab, as if you were a cat probing a goldfish bowl. You had gasped at the illusion that your kayak was not floating on water at all, but suspended vertiginously in the air over some surreal pseudo-aquatic landscape.

In a nutshell, what the limnologist—an expert in freshwater ecosystems—told you is that

Lake Malawi, the ninth largest lake in the world at 12,000 square miles (as big as Connecticut and Massachusetts combined), is densely oxygenated, and that a layer of warm, clear water overlays the colder, more turbid water beneath, resulting in exceptional visibility near the surface.

That clarity, however amazing, might be a short-lived fascination if not for the world it reveals. For Lake Malawi is home to more species of fish than any other lake in the world—almost 500 known, and perhaps as many not yet described—in colors and patterns that beggar any artist's palette. They range in size from large perch, carp, and bream, down to flickering, finned gemstones that could swim through a wedding ring.

Most of this staggering diversity derives from just one family of fish, the cichlids, a group that seems to possess a talent for adaptive radiation that would put Darwin's finches in the shade. From a presumed single ancestor, the cichlids in Lake Malawi have diversified to fill every conceivable niche and exploit every aquatic habitat. Over 400 species of cichlid are known in the lake, and

of these all but five are endemic; that is, they are found nowhere in the world except Lake Malawi. Even among the other fish found here, endemism is high: 29 species are known to only this lake. The cichlids of Lake Malawi are famous around the world among serious aquarium owners, who strive to include as many Malawian species as possible in their collections.

The subaquatic wonderland of Lake Malawi would make it a splendid paddling destination no matter where it was; that it lies in the heart of the African bush adds an overpowering sense of the exotic—and another world to explore above the surface. Giant baobab trees, looking as though they were planted upside down with trunks 15 or 20 feet in diameter, form imposing landmarks on the shore and on many of the islands in the lake. Beneath them, grazing on rocky outcroppings, you can spot bushbuck—small, reddish bovines with white stripes and short, spiral horns—and klipspringer—tiny, pug-faced antelope with straight horns. Hippos snort and bellow in the reed marshes, ignored by silent crocodiles.

AT A GLANCE

TRIP LENGTH 7–8 days	PRICE RANGE (INDEPENDENT TRIP) $190–$425
PADDLING DISTANCE 25–40 miles	PRICE RANGE (OUTFITTED GROUP TRIP)
PHYSICAL CHALLENGE ① 2 3 4 5	$750–$850
MENTAL CHALLENGE ① 2 3 4 5	STAGING CITY Lilongwe, Malawi
PRIME TIME June–September	HEADS UP Travel on east (Mozambique) side of lake not recommended

Lake Malawi, the ninth largest in the world, is home to almost 500 species of fish and a few adventurous kayakers.

Seemingly oblivious to the crocs are sacred ibises, stout-looking wading birds, and the comical jacanas, with feet as big as their bodies that enable them to walk over floating vegetation and lily pads. In the trees, African fish eagles punctuate dawn with their descending calls, and brilliant malachite kingfishers watch for small fish to venture too close to the surface. Now and then, although this is not ideal terrain for them, an elephant appears on shore. And always, the omnipresent vervet monkeys watch for opportunities to make mischief and steal food.

Lake Malawi is almost 400 miles long, relatively narrow, and very deep—over 2,000 feet in places. For thousands of years humans have lived along its shores, drinking its water and eating its fish (today the lake produces 40,000 tons annually, 70 percent of the animal protein consumed in Malawi, although population growth is stressing this). In 1980, a 22,000-acre national park was established at the southern end of the lake, on a peninsula that thrusts northward to form two enormous bays on either side. Unlike many parks in Africa and elsewhere, however, the officials who set up Lake Malawi National Park recognized the intrinsic rights of the people who already lived there. As a result, five native villages exist within the park boundaries, the residents of which still fish in the lake (with limits on certain species and methods) and make additional money selling crafts, especially beautifully woven straw hats and toys, to the tourists who come to dive in the clear water.

It's easy to see the dilemma faced by Third World administrators in managing a resource as precious as Lake Malawi. It would be easy to succumb to the temptation of big money, and kick all the villagers out to allow giant resorts exclusive access to the lake, or to allow unrestricted commercial fishing. That this is not (yet) the case here is encouraging, although there is increasing resort development near the national park and along the west shore of the lake.

Paddling silently along the shore of a forested island, beneath tall borasus palm trees, watching for otters playing among the boulders, you'll find yourself praying the Malawians can balance their desperate need for foreign capital with the chance to preserve this place humans have used for millenia, yet so far avoided spoiling. Sitting on the shore under the stars, watching the glimmering reflection from the constellations on the water, and the flickering lanterns on the fishermen's boats as they cast nets for the small fish called *usipa*, you'll hope this small slice of the old Africa will persist, as it has since long before David Livingstone witnessed the same scene 150 years ago and christened Malawi "The Lake of Stars."

Communicating isn't a problem; English is one of Malawi's two official languages. A few words of Chichewa are also handy.

SUGGESTED ROUTES

To explore Lake Malawi National Park, you can launch from several villages on the Nankumba Peninsula, such as Nkopola on the east side, or farther north in Monkey Bay, closer to the busy tourist area of Cape Maclear at the tip of the peninsula. There are several resorts along this stretch, with guests mindlessly indulging in the

AFRICAN FISH EAGLES

With its handsome dark brown and gray body and snow-white head, you could easily take the African fish eagle for a North American bald eagle. But the white on the fish eagle extends farther down on its chest, forming a larger hood (the two are in the same genus, *Haliaeetus*, however).

The fish eagle's specific name, *vocifer*, offers a clue as to another clear difference between the two: fish eagles are highly vocal, and their descending call is one of the signature sounds of the African dawn, or any other time of day for that matter. They are found continent-wide south of the Sahara, wherever there are fish.

Like the bald eagle, the fish eagle subsists largely on fish, both caught and scavenged, and occasionally stolen from other birds, but will now and then take small mammals or good-sized birds.

Just as with bald eagles, fish eagles are easy to spot from far away once you learn to look for that little white dot sitting out on a bare branch above a river or lake. Long after you leave Africa, you'll be able to play that call back in your head.

Kayak Africa, a South African tour operator, rents Klepper folding kayaks that can be rigged with a sail.

identical sorts of activities promoted by resorts around the world: hanging from giant parasails, zipping back and forth on jet skis, that kind of thing. Paddle offshore to the islands: Boadzulu, Domwe, Mambo, Maleri, Thumb West. All have beaches suitable for landing and camping.

If you're on your own and want to get away from the main tourist facilities, you can launch from the west shore of the lake, for example at Chipoka, and travel north. But remember that this is not wilderness in the sense we know it in the west; there are people living along the shore in villages and small compounds. You learn to think of humans as rightful inhabitants of the habitat here, a concept that has been all but lost in the United States in our rush to, first, urbanize and, second, promote a "look, don't touch" attitude toward nature. The most remote stretch of shore on the Malawi side of the lake is between Nkhata Bay and Chitimba, where the north/south highway turns inland for about 80 miles. The coast is steeper here, with scattered bays and villages, and recommended if you are experienced and self-sufficient.

You could also paddle up the east shore of the lake, on the Mozambique side, which is nearly roadless and deserted. However, Mozambique is still recovering from decades of civil war, and people in small, silent boats could easily have their intentions misinterpreted. So traveling this part of the lake is probably not recommended at this writing, unless you're part of a confident group.

While the water may be fresh and warm, Lake Malawi should be treated like an ocean.

THE MOST MEMORABLE BIRD IN THE WORLD

Well, that's probably different for everyone, but I know what mine was. The pennant-winged nightjar belongs to a widespread family of insectivorous birds that hunt at dusk or at night, often by sitting quietly in an open area—which frequently means a road—and flying straight up to snatch insects as they fly past. You often see them rising up in the headlight beams on country roads, and that's where I saw my first pennant-winged nightjar, in front of a Land Cruiser on a dirt track in Zambia.

But, as you might suspect from its name, the pennant-winged nightjar is different from all its relatives. During breeding season, the males grow two primary wing feathers out to a length of 15 inches or more, which flutter rapidly behind them as they fly up in the light, like ribbons shivering in a high wind. I was lucky enough to see four of them on that trip, one caught by our tracker in a handheld spotlight, so we could watch the bird flutter for endless seconds until it rose out of reach of the beam.

Setting up camp on Likomo Island beneath a baobob tree; their trunks reach diameters of 20 feet.

Southerly winds can push steep, fast-moving waves over six feet high within a few minutes, and create dangerous surf on rocky shores. Plan long crossings with care. Unfortunately, you'll have difficulty getting any reliable radio weather reports; advice from local fishermen will be more trustworthy.

The lakeshore in the south is a mixture of boulders interspersed with stretches of pebble or sand beach; you'll rarely have trouble finding a landing spot. Tides are obviously not a factor (actually the lake does have tides, but they are too small to notice), so you can pitch your tent right on the beach, but keep in mind wind-driven surf. The water in the lake is potable, but should be filtered, treated with iodine, or boiled

before drinking. Bilharzia (schistosomiasis) is present in the lake, caused by minute worms that typically infest snails common in weedy areas along the shore. When the worms infest a human host they can cause anemia and kidney damage. Keep away from such areas when swimming or collecting water.

WHAT TO EXPECT

Buses regularly ply the road between the capital and airport hub of Lilongwe and the southern end of Lake Malawi. Take the Coachline buses if you feel the need for first-class service, but if you want a genuine African experience, take the InterCity buses. Pure chaos. You can also find rides with the pickups that ferry people and goods between

A typical Malawian dugout canoe (top) and the fishermen who use them (above) selling fish.

Chichewa to break the ice.

Do I need to tell you to bring all your kayaking equipment with you? Sea kayaking has yet to become a popular sport among the inhabitants of Malawi, which has one of the lowest per capita incomes in the world. The only alternative to taking your own boat—preferably a folder—would be to buy one of the beautiful locally made dugout canoes. They're heavy and not too stable, but admittedly can carry a lot of gear.

Lilongwe, a city of about 75,000 about 100 miles by road from the park, has numerous grocery stores for provisioning. You can also buy produce at native markets, but beware before you try shopping there: Third World standards of hygiene are dramatically different from what you're used to. You should probably buy only things you plan to cook. There is also a supermarket and bakery in Monkey Bay.

People in Malawi, as elsewhere in Africa, are genuinely delighted by travelers, especially once you get away from the tourist traps. You might be asked to visit someone's home and share a meal, in which case you can return the hospitality with small gifts: a bag of salt, sewing needles, pocket knives, inexpensive digital watches, or medium-sized fish hooks. Children love balloons, candy, and kazoos. A wonderful item to bring to trade for more valuable crafts is a multi-tool, such as a Leatherman.

Malaria is present in Malawi, and you must take medication to prevent it, beginning two weeks before your journey and continuing (depending on the drug) for several weeks afterward. The Centers for Disease Control recommend Larium, which is effective but has unpleasant side effects. Find a doctor who is familiar with malaria prophylactics and ask his or her advice. The best way to avoid malaria is to avoid being bitten by *Anopheles* mosquitoes. Use a screened tent for sleeping, and wear long pants, long-sleeved shirts, and insect repellent, especially near dusk.

towns, for a small fee. English is one of the official languages of Malawi, so you'll have little trouble communicating. However, you should definitely buy a phrase book and try to learn a few words of

Cape Maclear, at the tip of Nankumba Peninsula.

GUIDES AND OUTFITTERS

Kayak Africa runs several different trips in and around Lake Malawi National Park, from seven to eight days in length. Some trips include kayaking and snorkeling, others also include scuba diving and instruction. Costs are all-inclusive from Lilongwe. Kayak Africa also rents Klepper kayaks by the day and week.

KAYAK AFRICA

1 Salford Rd.
Mowbray, Cape Town, South Africa 7700
27-21-689-8123
www.kayakafrica.co.za
$750–$850 for 7–8 days

RECOMMENDED READING

■ *A BOAT IN OUR BAGGAGE,* Maria Coffey (1994. A Little, Brown.) A wonderful, insightful account of a couple's journey around the world with a folding kayak. It's out of print, but available from used bookstores.
■ *GUIDE TO MALAWI,* Philip Briggs (1999. $16.95. Bradt Publications.) A very thorough guide to the country.

Kadavu

Quite simply, a paddle through paradise.

Native children paddle a homemade kayak made from roofing tin.

P addling through paradise can be disarming. It's easy to lose all sense that, at certain times and places, sea kayaking requires a modicum of vigilance to be done safely. But it's hard to stay vigilant when you're floating on 75°F water in 80°F sunshine, with the surface of the lagoon barely rippling in a light southeasterly trade breeze. You look down through the water to the white sand only five or six feet down, where purple starfish lie scattered about like a photographic negative of the heavens. Your boat glides over the edge of a wide coral bed, and you can see butterfly fish flickering in and out of staghorn formations, and even make out some clown fish folded safely into the tentacles of brightly colored anenomes. The breeze rustles the fronds in the coconut palms overhanging the smooth, clean beach on your left, inviting a nap later on. Beyond the palms, green hills rise to volcanic peaks, each capped with a wisp of cloud

FIJI

VANUA LEVU

KORO SEA

Nadi VITI LEVU

Suva

KADAVU

Vunisea

SOUTH PACIFIC

that promises a shower by evening.

Yep, it's disarming—so when a 30-foot-square patch of the sea erupts in froth just off your bow, you're jolted into a decidedly uncoordinated state of alarm. In a heartbeat, several unlikely explanations zip through your head. *Shark? Manta? Volcanic eruption?* Then you see dozens of small, silvery blue shapes rocketing away on the surface. *Flying fish.* Jeez. Even the red alerts here are benign. Perhaps it's time for a lunch break to recuperate. An hour or two in the shade of a mango tree, some fresh fish ceviche with a lot of lime, a papaya, some fresh coconut milk—that should restore the equilibrium.

Given that they were describing a place that could easily pass as Eden, early European accounts of Fiji were far from lavish in their praise—at least regarding the indigenous population. American naval officer Charles Wilkes called the inhabitants "the most barbarous and savage race now existing upon the globe" when he visited in 1840. An English missionary claimed that "atrocities of the most fearful kind have come to my knowledge,

which I dare not record here." These observers were understandably perturbed—at least from the point of view of their own society—at witnessing not only habitual cannibalism, but gruesome rituals such as that involving the christening of new 90-foot war canoes by launching them over the lined-up bodies of young women.

The Europeans who began settling in Fiji in the 19th century put an end to the cannibalism and most rituals, while introducing benefits of their own culture such as venereal disease and measles (the latter killed 20 percent of the Fijian population in 1875). They also tried to introduce blackbirding—a system of indentured servitude that in practice more closely resembled slavery—to force native Fijians to work on sugarcane plantations. When the natives reacted petulantly to this, often by attacking the plantation owners, the British colonial government banned the practice and began substituting laborers from India, with the historical result that today nearly half of Fiji's population is of Indian descent, thoroughly confusing first-time travelers with scenes of sari-clad

---

AT A GLANCE

TRIP LENGTH 7–10 days

PADDLING DISTANCE About 80 miles for a circumnavigation of Kadavu

PHYSICAL CHALLENGE ① ② 3 4 5

MENTAL CHALLENGE ① ② 3 4 5

PRIME TIME May–October, winter in the Southern Hemisphere, when the weather is generally warm and relatively dry

PRICE RANGE (INDEPENDENT TRIP) $775–$1,350

PRICE RANGE (OUTFITTED GROUP TRIP) $1,000–$2,550

STAGING CITY Nadi, Fiji

HEADS UP Check State Department warnings regarding travel safety. At press time there was some political turmoil.

Above: *A slice of paradise— fresh pineapple in the shade of palms overhanging the beach. Opposite: Paddling off into the sunset from Taveuni Island.*

women strolling past Hindu and Muslim temples.

Fortunately for modern tourists, Fiji's sanguinary past is behind it (although islanders are known to tease visitors by pinching their arms and declaring "Not ready yet!"). In fact, Fijians have a traditional and very formal system for welcoming strangers, involving the exchange of gifts and the drinking of a mildly narcotic beverage called *yaqona* (kava elsewhere in the Pacific), made from the ground roots of a pepper plant of the same name (and now available in some herbal medicine outlets in the United States). A supply of *yaqona* root bundles to present to village headmen is still a basic hospitality item for independent travelers in Fiji. But it's not all formality—Fijians on the street are quite possibly the most cheerful people in the world, with a ready smile for anyone. The standard greeting is a hearty "Bula!" ("Health!").

Most people think of Fiji as one island, but it actually comprises over 300, the largest two of which are also where the majority of Fiji's 750,000 people live, and where most of the giant piña-colada-by-the-pool resorts are. Though all the islands are volcanic in origin, subsequently

FIJIAN ETIQUETTE

Fijians are far too polite to show offense to foreigners who are ignorant of local customs, but you will gain tremendous goodwill by being prepared in advance.

In Fijian villages, only chiefs are allowed to wear hats and sunglasses; take yours off before entering, and ask before wandering around the village to gawk. Both women and men should carry a light sarong to wear over a bathing suit, and should always remove footwear before entering a hut.

If you are invited to a *yaqona* ceremony, you will sit in a circle on mats inside a hut. Sit with your legs crossed; never point the bottoms of your feet at anyone. If you are with a tour, your leader will offer a gift to the host, generally a bundle of *yaqona* roots. A bowl of *yaqona* will be returned. The person receiving the bowl claps once, takes the bowl in both hands, and drains it at one pass (*yaqona* has a slightly bitter taste of earth or sawdust), after which everyone claps three times. As the bowl is refilled and passed to succeeding guests the clapping is repeated. Everyone remains silent through the ceremony except for those giving formal speeches. That's just as well, you'll discover, since *yaqona* has a distinct numbing effect on the lips and tongue.

Life on the water is relaxed; you rarely encounter winds over 20 knots or waves over a couple of feet.

augmented by coral formation, they were formed at different times and so vary remarkably in appearance. Some, such as Viti Levu and Vanua Levu, the big islands, still boast tall inland peaks, while other islands are low and flat, composed almost entirely of coral. The diverse structure has resulted in a stunning diversity of life as well, fertilized by the nutrient-rich upwelling from the deep Tonga Trench. This is probably the best place in the world to see soft corals, especially on the Rainbow Reef in the Somosomo Strait between Vanua Levu and Taveuni. Other well-known sites are the Great White Wall, the Beqa Lagoon, and Astrolabe Reef off the Kadavu Group of islands. Snorkeling gear should be mandatory equipment on sea kayaks in Fiji.

Sixty miles south of Viti Levu and the Fijian capital of Suva lies the Kadavu Group of islands, consisting of one main island plus a half-dozen small ones. Here, far from the international airport and the main concentration of resorts, life proceeds at a pace more like what one would expect in a South Seas paradise. Only a few lodges do business on Kadavu, catering mostly to divers; other than that, there are only native villages scattered along the coast. This unspoiled atmosphere makes the island a natural for kayakers seeking the real Fiji experience—unhurried, uncrowded, and uncomplicated.

On the short flight out from Nadi International Airport on Viti Levu, Kadavu's green mountains rise out of the sea like the Lost World, dramatically isolated in an expanse of deep blue ocean. Fringing reefs and lagoons glow in mottled shades of turquoise, and brilliant white sand etches a fine border between sea and forest. The residents are genuinely delighted by visitors, exhibiting a curiosity that goes beyond simple friendliness. The islanders still gather most of their living from the land and sea, eating fish, mango, coconut, papaya, wild citrus, a few cultivated crops such as sweet potato, and chicken and pork. Stuccoed houses tend toward bright colors— reflecting the general attitude toward life—and a few still boast thatched roofs (although most have the more hurricane-resistant galvanized metal).

Life on the water around Kadavu is just as relaxed as life on the beach. It's rare to have to deal with winds over 20 miles per hour or waves over a couple of feet (if you stay inside the fringing reef). This is not a place for daily mileage goals; if any members of your group try to impose a schedule they should immediately be keelhauled, or forced to tow everyone else for several hours.

Paddling Fiji makes you fully empathize with the *Bounty* mutineers. It's extemely easy to slide into that carefree island existence and wind up wondering why on earth you waste time on a nine-to-five job back home. However, I must warn you that there is a genuine danger involved in messing around in Fiji. A number of people—and I am not making this up—have been injured by falling coconuts while lounging under palm trees. So check out that nap site carefully.

SUGGESTED ROUTES

Kadavu, about 160 square miles in area, comprises three hilly sections connected by two narrow isthmuses. The airstrip is located on the southern isthmus, in the village of Vunisea. You can paddle directly from the dock in Galoa Harbor, on the southeast side of the isthmus, but it's also possible to arrange a ride to another seaside village, such as Ravitaki or Muani with one of the small commercial trucks that distribute supplies along the 40 miles of dirt road on the island (there are no buses).

Top: Native spear fisherman. Above: Plotting a course.
Overleaf: In Fiji, it's easy to slide into a carefree island existence and contemplate postponing your return indefinitely.

"Fijians on the street are possibly the most cheerful people in the world."

ask for permission to camp nearby. You'll invariably be greeted by a mob of laughing, shouting children (who might just follow you to your camp nearby).

Another really good strategy is to arrange a stay at one of the pleasing, and very modest, dive resorts on Kadavu, and do day trips from there. One of the closest to the airstrip is Reece's Place, on Galoa Island, just a short hop from the dock in Vunisea. A couple more, Albert's Place and the Nukubalavu Adventure Resort, are on the northern tip of Kadavu, adjacent to the magnificent Astrolabe Reef. They can arrange boat transfers from either the Kadavu airstrip or directly from Suva, on Viti Levu. All these places offer simple, thatched accommodations and meals, very much in keeping with the south seas idyll.

It would be feasible to do a complete circumnavigation of Kadavu (about 80 miles) in a week or two. However, to leave more time for snorkeling and lounging, you can do what a couple of the commercial tour companies do and just paddle around the southern lobe of the island, camping on deserted beaches and the small Matanuku Island off the southern coast. Or you can stop at the villages that peek out of the palms along the shore—Buelevu, Nabukelevuira, Lomati, Tavuki, or others—and

WHAT TO EXPECT

Weather during the Southern Hemisphere winter is normally mild and warm, with occasional showers. Rainfall tends to be less on the leeward (northwest) side of the large islands; you can see distinct vegetation differences on Viti Levu, but not so much on Kadavu. There are fewer tourists during the austral summer (November through March), but rainfall is high and there is

PRONOUNCING FIJIAN WORDS

Visitors to Fiji notice that spoken words often sound different from their written counterparts. When Fijian was first translated into English spelling in 1835, by a missionary named David Cargill, he took into account the fact that to Fijians many single letters are pronounced as consonants. Visitors can master most pronunciation by remembering a few simple rules.

The letter b is pronounced with an m in front of it, as in the word amber.

The letter d is pronounced with an n in front of it, as in gender.

The letter g is pronounced with a soft n in front, as in song.

The letter c is pronounced th.

The letter q is pronounced as a hard ng. *Yaqona* is pronounced *yangona*.

It seems confusing at first, but you soon pick up the gist of at least the common consonants. In fact, the most difficult trick is dropping the habit when you return home.

a chance of hurricanes.

Prevailing trade winds in Kadavu are generally from the southeast. They're usually light (under 20 knots) in winter, but can kick up occasionally. Fortunately, most open-ocean wave action is broken by the barrier reefs. Tidal range is only a few feet on Kadavu, and currents are generally not a concern.

There are kayaks to be found for rent in Fiji, but mostly of the sit-on-top variety, suitable more for day trips than touring (although I hear some shops are carrying folding kayaks). It's best to bring your own paddling gear. However, you'll have no trouble provisioning in towns on the big islands.

You won't need immersion protection here. Clothing for Fiji should be lightweight and offer full sun coverage. Long-sleeved nylon shirts and long pants dry quickly but prevent sunburn. Cotton works just fine too, but you'll stay wet longer.

GUIDES AND OUTFITTERS

Tamarillo Expeditions in New Zealand offers an eight-day tour of Kadavu, all-inclusive from Nadi. Kayak Kadavu has an eight-day tour of Kadavu.

TAMARILLO EXPEDITIONS

P.O. Box 9869
Wellington, New Zealand
0064-4-801-7549
www.tamarillo.co.nz
$1,000 for 8 days

KAYAK KADAVU

888-593-3454
www.mavi.net/~kayak/fiji
$3,100 for 8 days from L.A.

RECOMMENDED READING

■ *BLUE HORIZONS: PARADISE ISLES OF THE PACIFIC,* Ron Fisher et al (1985. National Geographic Society. Out of print.) Good introduction to the people and history of the region.

Most open-ocean wave action is broken by barrier reefs.

■ *ADVENTURING IN THE PACIFIC,* Susanna Margolis (1995. $16.00. Sierra Club Books.) Tips oriented toward the independent traveler.
■ *FROMMER'S SOUTH PACIFIC,* Bill Goodwin (1998. $19.95. Macmillan Travel.) Decent general guide to travel in the South Pacific.

The Rock Islands

Gardens in the sea—lush islands and turquoise water—lent poignancy by the ghosts of past conflict.

The best sea kayaking trips (indeed, the best of any kind of trip) can be replayed in your mind like a well-remembered film. But there are almost always a few vignettes that stand out with extra clarity, as though the film had been frozen on one perfect frame in a flash of light. I think of those vignettes as defining moments, since they capture the essence of the entire trip in a brief burst of total recall—not only the sights, but the sounds, smells, and tastes seem to flood the memory. These moments can bring back many different moods, from outright joy to fear, to introspection, to something even deeper.

Picture yourself stroking slowly into a glassy lagoon toward a small coral islet. About 50 feet across, its rounded peak is densely vegetated with shrubs, vines, and short palm trees. But wave action combined with uplifting has drastically undercut the base of the islet, so that the whole

Rock formations off Babeldaob, by far the largest island in Palau.

thing balances improbably on a pedestal perhaps 15 feet thick. Scattered around the lagoon are a half-dozen similar apparitions, looking like giant arrangements of house plants in top-heavy pots.

As you approach the shallow water surrounding the islet, something in the water beneath your kayak catches your eye, and you look down. Directly underneath you, sitting eerily intact and upright, its outlines only minimally blurred by encrusting growth, is an airplane—a 60-year-old Japanese floatplane, sunk by the United States Army Air Force during the bloody fighting that raged on and around Peleliu, at the southern end of Palau, in 1944.

Think for a moment about the Corsairs screaming in off the aircraft carriers, dropping torpedoes and rending water and earth with bullets from their .50 caliber guns, while the landing craft land wave after wave of troops on the beaches of Peleliu, where 2,000 Americans and 11,000 Japanese would die. Look around again—at the blue sky, the calm water, the tiny tropical islands balanced on their delicate stems. Smell the sweet sea breeze, and hear the foliage rustle, the wavelets that slurp at the undercut coral, even the chitinous scurrying of the emerald crabs.

That's what I call a defining moment.

THE REPUBLIC OF PALAU (*Belau* to the inhabitants), part of the Micronesian chain of islands, lies seven degrees north of the equator, about 800 miles southwest of Guam. The origins of the 350 islands in the Palau archipelago are not fully understood; they may still be developing into what geologists call an island arc—a semicircular grouping caused by lifting and tilting. The largest, Babeldaob, covers 152 square miles and is the second largest island in Micronesia after Guam; the rest of the Palauan islands are much smaller (the entire republic is less than 200 square miles). Fringing and barrier reefs shelter most of the chain from ocean waves (although the tidal range in some places can reach over six and a half feet).

The underwater world of Palau, a spectacular seascape of blue holes, thousand-foot drop-offs, and sunken planes and ships, has been known for decades to sport divers. But the dive

---

AT A GLANCE

TRIP LENGTH 7–10 days	PRICE RANGE (INDEPENDENT TRIP) $175–$500
PADDLING DISTANCE 30–100 miles	PRICE RANGE (OUTFITTED GROUP TRIP)
PHYSICAL CHALLENGE ①② 3 4 5	$50–$1,600
MENTAL CHALLENGE ①② 3 4 5	STAGING CITY Koror, Palau
PRIME TIME February–April, October–December	

boats usually take the shortest route through the islands to get to the most popular scuba sites—leaving open a whole universe of exploration for the sea kayaker. And because of the clustered distribution of the islands, and the protective reef, access is easy.

The capital of Palau, Koror, perches on a small island of the same name just off the southern tip of Babeldaob—in fact, Koror's airport is on Babeldaob, and visitors transfer by bus or taxi over a bridge. Koror looks south over a sheltered harbor toward the Rock Islands, a cluster numbering about 200 that stretches in a south-southwest direction for 25 miles to the end of the reef—and the large island of Peleliu, where the Japanese holed up in a labyrinth of limestone caves to fight an American invasion that many military historians consider pointless (the island was of little or no strategic value, and the Japanese garrison there would have been helpless to stem the tide of the American recapture of truly vital territory).

Even to a nonscientist, it's apparent that Palau is a different world both geologically and botanically from the Polynesian Islands farther east in the Pacific. The recent (and probably ongoing) tilting and settling of the Palauan chain has contributed to a variety of island

Above: Young Palauan girl on a dock in the village of Ngaraard, east coast of Babeldaob. Opposite: Exploring the Rock Islands. From a distance they appear as an unbroken green line; as you draw near, they separate into dozens of individual mounds.

MICRONESIA, MELANESIA, POLYNESIA—WHERE THE HECK AM I?

It's easy to get confused by the different regions of the southwestern Pacific Ocean. And since the original seafaring peoples for whom the regions are named frequently mixed with, conquered, and succeeded each other, the lines are blurred. But the general outlines are easy to define.

Melanesia, which was the first to be settled (beginning as early as 50,000 years ago) includes New Guinea, Fiji, and an arc of islands off the northeast coast of Australia. The people who first came here were dark-skinned relatives of Australia's Aborigines. Melanesia today is by far the largest Pacific region, with 95 percent of the land area and 70 percent of the population.

A second wave of migration originated in Southeast Asia about 5,000 years ago and occupied what we now call Micronesia, a swath of islands north of Melanesia including Palau, the Marianas, and the Marshall Islands. These people were of Indonesian stock, lighter-skinned than the Melanesians.

Polynesia was the last part of the world to be permanently colonized by man. These scattered islands in the central southern Pacific were first reached by an offshoot of the Micronesian culture traced by a particular type of pottery known as Lapita. The region developed its own culture and traditions, and its people eventually reached and settled such isolated island chains as Hawaii and Easter Island.

Gorgonian sea fan. The sea is so clear you can see the bottom 75 feet below, and there is plenty to see: the waters are home to 1,500 fish species.

geography here, including spectacular natural arches, sea caves, vertical bluffs of limestone, and the overhanging "mushroom cap" islets. The vegetation crowding the tops of the islands resembles a Southeast Asian jungle more than a South Seas palm and mango forest. There is also evidence of the different peoples who settled the Micronesian region. On Ulong, one of the westernmost Rock Islands, is a well-preserved set of rock paintings, and some village sites nearby have been carbon dated to 1000 B.C. More recently, Ulong provided a refuge for the crew of a British ship, the H.M.S. *Antelope*, which foundered on the barrier reef in 1783.

Unlike similar idyllic getaways, paddling in Palau offers the thinking kayaker much food for introspection. The yin and yang of a lush paradise scattered throughout with reminders of a brutal war adds a serious dimension to the surroundings, and fosters a level of deep appreciation possibly unmatched by any other place on earth.

SUGGESTED ROUTES

There's no need for shuttles or charters to paddle the Rock Islands—you just launch out of the harbor in Koror. From the cockpit of a kayak, the islands appear as an unbroken green line

CORAL BLEACHING

In late 1998, a persistent El Niño kept the ocean water around Palau, as well as many other areas of the western Pacific, above 90°F for several weeks. Such sustained high temperatures greatly stressed the surrounding coral reefs, and the result was a phenomenon known as coral bleaching.

Coral exists in a symbiotic relationship with unicellular plants called zooxanthellae, which live in the surface tissues of the coral polyps. The zooxanthellae, through photosynthesis, provide the coral with oxygen,

and digest much of the cellular waste of the coral. The zooxanthellae in return benefit from a stable, protected environment and abundant nutrients.

Corals gain much of their color from the symbiotic zooxanthellae—but when subjected to prolonged temperature stress, as in 1998, the corals will expel the zooxanthellae, leaving reefs with a colorless, bleached appearance. Once sea temperatures return to normal, the coral will be recolonized by zooxanthellae, but the process can take years.

Seventy Islands, part of the Rock Islands. Hundreds of these "mushroom cap" islets, each around 50 feet across and covered with dense vegetation, dot the sea south of Koror, the capital.

blocking the horizon, and gradually separate into dozens of individual mounds as you draw near. One narrow, 15-mile-long island forms a giant, northwest-facing cradle sheltering dozens of small islands in its embrace.

There are absolutely no established routes through the Rock Islands—the majority of which aren't even named—but the farther away you venture from the direct line from Koror to Peleliu, the fewer dive boats you'll see zipping past at 30 knots. Almost all crossings are short, often no more than a hundred yards, and the water is rarely rough enough to preclude paddling.

The small group of islands farthest west in the chain, Ulong, has several spectacular beaches and some well-preserved rock paintings. As you paddle between the islands, watch for rare dugongs (similar to manatees), of which fewer than 200 are left in Palau. You'll also occasionally spot a small shark that has made it through the barrier reef. But don't forget to look up and watch for the giant fruit bats hanging in trees near the water's edge.

The total distance from Koror to Peleliu is only about 30 miles, but you can easily triple that wandering about here and there.

WHAT TO EXPECT

It's a long haul from the United States to Palau—nine hours from Honolulu to Guam, then three more to Koror—so be prepared for some jet lag recuperation in Koror.

Koror (population about 10,000) has

The Rock Islands, some 200 of them, stretch south-southwest from Koror to Peleliu, 25 miles away.

groceries and other basic supplies. U. S. currency and English are standard here, since Palau only gained its independence in 1994.

Koror has more than its share of resorts, most of them right on the water, and prices tend to be surprisingly good owing to the competition and packages they offer. A good resource is the World of Diving website (www.worldofdiving.com), which lists a half-dozen resorts with options for all-inclusive stays. Some are reasonable enough that you could just book one and skip the diving part.

Palau is known for some of the clearest water in the world. I'm impressed when I can look down from my kayak and see the bottom through 30 feet of water—here you can do it at 75 feet. And the clarity increases when you drop over the side with a mask: 200 feet of horizontal visibility is common. Palau's proximity to the rich Indo-Malay faunal region is apparent as you snorkel across shallow coral lagoons, around the undercut bases of the islets, or over the vertiginous drop-offs: there are more than 1,500 species of fish here, and hundreds of species of soft coral and anemones. And, of course, the odd warplane.

Water temperature averages in the 80s (F)— in Palau—dress to prevent sun exposure. Mosquitoes and sand flies are present, but usually not too troublesome. There is no malaria present.

Landing sites in the Rock Islands tend to be either yes or no. Either you're faced with an over-hanging mushroom, a sheer limestone bluff, or a gently sloping sandy beach. Some of the islands are technically off-limits; ask at the dive shops and tour operators in Koror for directions.

Let's see—what else? Um . . .Rats. Escapees from centuries of ship landings and wrecks, rats are common nocturnal pests on many of the islands. They'll steal your food if you don't tie it in bags from trees, and skitter over you while you sleep if you don't use a tent. Otherwise, however, they're harmless, as are the two native species of snakes in Palau. More impressive, but equally harmless, are the monitor lizards that grow to around three feet in length. In the mangrove swamps on the big island of Babeldaob, on the other hand, the crocodiles can be 15 feet long and have been known to snag the odd *Homo sapiens*. But you've little reason to be kayaking there anyway.

There is no reliable drinking water on the Rock Islands; if you go during the dry season you'll have to carry your own or arrange for resupply—easy to do with one of the charter companies in Koror.

There is no reliable drinking water on the Rock Islands; if you go during the dry season you'll have to carry your own or arrange for resupply.

GUIDES AND OUTFITTERS

KAYAK CONNECTION
831-724-5692
2370 Highway 1
Moss Landing, CA 95039
$1,600 for 9 days, all-inclusive

PALAU KAYAK TOURS
P.O. Box 1714-P105
Koror, Republic of Palau, 96940
680-488-5885
$500 for 7 days

RECOMMENDED READING

■ *LONELY PLANET MICRONESIA,* Kate Galbraith (2000. $15.95. Lonely Planet Guides.) Full of useful information.

■ *THE DEVIL'S ANVIL: THE ASSAULT ON PELELIU,* James Hallas (1994. $28.50. Praeger.) Must-read account of the costly invasion of Palau during World War II.

Daytrips

The River Thames

he Thames is far from being a major world river from a geographical perspective: It's barely more than 200 miles long from source to sea. But its importance as a conduit of human history far outstrips its physical dimensions.

The modern Thames is divided into two sections: the tidal and the nontidal. Above Kingston (toward the western edge of the London metropolitan area), locks prevent tidal forces from affecting the river, and also slow its flow, so boat-

ing in the upper stretches of the river is serene—hence the regattas at Henley and rowing at Oxford. Below Kingston the twice-daily tidal bore still determines when and where both large and small boats can go: Large craft must avoid grounding, and smaller boats must watch the current, which may flow strongly in the opposite direction one thinks the river should be moving. When the Romans founded Londinium in A.D. 45, they

found that the incoming tidal bore could carry them 50 miles inland against the current.

If you've got a spare day or two in England, and want to get a taste of the genteel boating life of the Thames, the place to go is Oxford. The scene on the river here could be a century old, as undergraduates from the university ply the calm water in rowing punts, with their dates riding elegantly in the stern.

The character of the Thames changes significantly at Oxford, specifically at Osney Bridge, which is too low to allow the triple-decker tour boats that are common downstream to pass under it. So the upper reaches of the river are the territory for smaller craft, including the charming live-aboard narrow boats, some of which are 70 feet long and only 7 feet wide, designed for negotiating the narrow inland canals of England. You can paddle upstream from Osney Bridge, where the river widens into farmland, and either turn around at Godstow Lock, or portage around it and continue to King's Lock, which is still manually operated. If you head downstream from Osney Bridge, you'll find expansive estates lining the river, with private wharves and acres of lawn. Whichever way you go, you'll never be far from a riverside pub and a filling meal of fish and chips washed down with a pint or two.

Paddling distance is approximately 3 to 12 miles.

Above: Royal Henley Regatta course, Henley-on-Thames, on the nontidal river.
Opposite: Big Ben and the Houses of Parliament from the River Thames in the heart of London.

The Maine Island Trail

Black granite sets off green spruce and fur, an osprey calls high above, and Down East hospitality awaits at the end of the day.

M any adventure sports have what might be called a signature route—a path somewhere in the world that, above all others, is linked inextricably with that sport, and which serious participants regard as something of a pilgrimage. For blue-water sailors it's the downwind tropical run from the Galapagos to the South Pacific Islands. Trekkers take the classic track from Kathmandu to Everest Base Camp, while backpackers tackle the Appalachian Trail, and cross-country skiers traverse the Haute Route.

My vote for the signature sea kayaking route goes to the Maine Island Trail.

If you straightened out the entire coast of Maine—barely 200 airline miles between Kittery on the border with New Hampshire and Eastport on the far eastern tip of the state—it would bridge the distance between New York City and Denver, Colorado. And that's not counting the coastline of Maine's 1,700 odd islands

Heading out for a paddle at sunset, Muskungus Bay, Maine Island Trail.

MAINE

Bar Harbor

Castine
Pepobscot Bay DEER ISLE MOUNT DESERT ISLAND

VINALHAVEN ISLAND ISLE AU HAUT

Caseo Bay GULF OF MAINE

Portland

that are big enough to support significant vegetation. Add it all up and it would stretch from the Big Apple to Los Angeles.

So there's a lot of coast in Maine. Yet the figures would be simply amusing statistics if that 3,000-plus miles wasn't possibly the most beautiful part of the entire east coast of the United States. It's a twisted, convoluted, folded shore that beckons a small boat pilot to explore just one more turn, to peek into one more bay, to see what's behind one more island—and also offers plenty of sheltered paddling and refuges from sudden weather changes. And Maine's beauty is divided equally between sea and land. The ancient, glacier-carved granite and schist that rise from the water are reassuring in their solidity, and saved from starkness by the cool green forests of spruce, fir, and oak that crowd their edges. Paddlers can watch seals and whales offshore; in the air you'll see ospreys (in greater density than anywhere else in my experience), bald eagles, and dozens of other species of sea, land, and shore birds. Self-sufficient paddlers can utilize hundreds of camping sites on the mainland and islands, yet the sybarite could easily arrange an inn-to-inn tour

and never pound a single tent stake.

The Maine coast boasts another rare quality: It's one of the very few places where villages and seaside homes seem to fit attractively into the landscape instead of spoiling it. I've guessed at reasons for this for years. Perhaps it's because so many of the houses are old, wood, modestly sized, and carefully tended, so they slot into their environment in a pleasingly organic fashion (in direct contrast to, say, some of the hey-look-at-me monstrosities along the California coast). Perhaps it stems from an extra respect for the ocean shared by the residents, a significant number of whom still make a living from the sea. Maybe it's just old-fashioned good taste, which would sneer at garish attempts to outdo nature. Whatever the reasons, rounding a point on the Maine coast and finding a tidy white clapboard cottage clinging to the side of a wooded hill often elicits remarks of delight (tinged with envy) rather than disappointment.

The dense profusion of islands (there are over 3,000 if you count bare rock), plus

Overleaf: Off Pemaquid Point lighthouse. Maine's rocky shore and surging surf make for tricky landings.

AT A GLANCE

TRIP LENGTH 1/2 day–6 weeks
PADDLING DISTANCE 2–325 miles
PHYSICAL CHALLENGE 1 ② ③ 4 5
MENTAL CHALLENGE ① ② 3 4 5
PRIME TIME June–August (most popular), September (my pick)

PRICE RANGE (INDEPENDENT TRIP) $325–$775
PRICE RANGE (OUTFITTED GROUP TRIP)
$45–$895
STAGING CITY Portland, Maine

uncounted inlets and bays, makes the Maine coast a dream route for paddlers of all skill levels. However, like any other destination there are local factors to be considered. Many islands are too small for camping; others are privately owned and off-limits. Tidal currents in many areas are a significant factor for kayakers, along with the occasional fogs that descend like a sudden case of blinding cataracts. Such considerations usually demand a lot of research and a bit of luck for a visiting sea kayaker. But not in Maine— anyone can visit here and paddle like a native, thanks to the Maine Island Trail Association (M.I.T.A.). Founded by David Getchell, the M.I.T.A. created and oversees a 325-mile waterway that starts in Portland and ends in Machias Bay. Along the trail are about 75 islands with designated campsites, 40 of which are state-owned, plus another 35 that are private, for M.I.T.A. members' use only. The association publishes an annual guidebook to the trail that contains everything for the visitor except current weather and tides (it includes mini-charts of the trail, but I suggest buying full-size charts of your planned route). Signing up for a membership in M.I.T.A. will net you most of the information you need for a tour of the best of the Maine coast. You can contact M.I.T.A. at 207-596-6456, P.O. Box C, Rockland, ME 04841.

It's perfectly possible to camp the entire length of the trail. But this is one paddling destination where I confess a strong attraction to a more sybaritic approach, to exploit what is likely the finest concentration of inns and B&Bs in the United States. Even if, like me, your happiest nights are spent camping miles from the nearest

Above: Kayak surfing off Pemaquid. Opposite: Heading for the lighthouse, Isle au Haut Bay, Isle au Haut.

OSPREYS

One of the most widely distributed fish-eating hawks in the world, the osprey seems particularly abundant in Maine. Ospreys are easy to identify once you spot the hawklike shape, as their dark wings contrast with a white chest and face, broken by a dark stripe extending back from the eye.

Ospreys circle the water or hover looking for fish just beneath the surface, then plunge feetfirst to snatch them. If their aim is true, they rise from the water and fly off to a perch or the nest with the fish turned head forward to minimize drag. Sometimes bald eagles steal their catch, diving on the osprey until it drops the fish, then swooping down to snatch it themselves.

Osprey nests are large accretions of sticks found high in trees that have bare or dead branches, especially firs in Maine. The nests are added to each year and can weigh hundreds of pounds. The birds are sensitive to intruders, and will screech petulantly at approaching kayakers. Don't land near osprey nests during the breeding season (April through July in Maine).

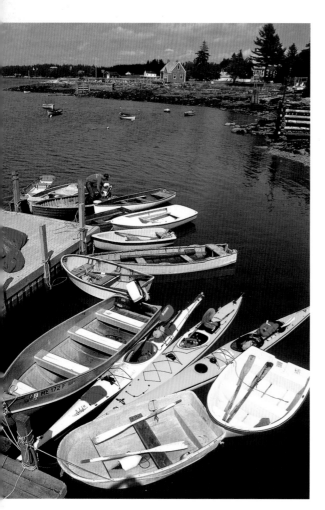

Dockside along the Maine Island Trail, Acadia National Park, Mount Desert Island.

human, an inn-to-inn tour—especially in the Penobscot Bay area—might be the most delightful way to experience three of the best things Maine has to offer: great hospitality, splendid ocean views, and the best seafood in the world.

But how do you justify this narcissistic indulgence when engaging in a sport that's supposed to be all about rugged challenges? I've already figured that out. You see, it's well known that a lightly loaded kayak—one without a tent, stove, or a lot of canned food in it—is easier to Eskimo roll in the event of a capsize. Therefore, all that luxury—

those warm beds, those pre-dinner cocktails, the lobster with wild mushrooms, that poached salmon with beurre blanc—is all suffered purely in the interest of safety.

SUGGESTED ROUTES

For many paddlers, the goal of traversing the entire 325 miles of the Maine Island Trail is irresistible. But for the first-time visitor with less than several weeks of free time, thoroughly exploring just a portion of the trail is more rewarding than simply trying to rack up mileage. There are several ports that make superb bases for weekend or weeklong trips—Camden or Bar Harbor, for example—but my favorite is the tiny port of Castine, on the northeast side of Penobscot Bay and right in the middle of the trail. Not only is Castine lovely, with many perfectly preserved 200-year-old buildings and a harbor dotted with moored sailboats, it is also the site of the L.L. Bean Sea Kayaking Symposium held each year in July, so a more kayak-friendly place would be hard to find. The little downtown harbor has both floating docks and a ramp, plus good overnight parking a block away, restrooms, even picnic tables (and an ice cream shop).

From Castine it's only a 2-mile hop south to the Holbrook Island Sanctuary and its outstanding birding. Beyond that are Deer Isle and Isle au Haut (pronounced quickly: ile-oh-hoe), and dozens of islands in between. Around Naskeag Point to the east are Swans Island and the enormous Mount Desert Island (pronounced like the after-dinner sweet), almost half of which is Acadia National Park and which boasts the only natural fjord on the east coast of the United States. Since there is a bridge to Mount Desert Island, by arranging a vehicle shuttle a group of friends can make an easy five- or six-day tour of this most classic section of the Maine coast, with no backtracking.

One sequence, including some of the best inns in the state, connects Castine with Isle au Haut. First is the Castine Inn, a carefully restored

In the cold waters and unpredictable weather along the Maine coast, it makes sense to paddle in pairs.

REVOLUTIONARY HISTORY

The Maine coast was the site of the first naval battle of the Revolutionary War, when colonials captured the British sloop *Margaretta* off Machias in 1775. By 1779, when the outcome of the revolt was still far from settled, Castine was a stronghold of British support and a refuge of sorts for Tories (British loyalists) who had fled from the upstart American colonies to the south. The British had begun construction of a fort named after King George, at which around 750 troops were stationed, along with a couple of small sloops. In a preemptive strike, the Commonwealth of Massachusetts sent a fleet of armed vessels and transports carrying nearly 1,500 troops to capture the town and fort. The fleet made it to Castine unopposed, but the American privateer commanders delayed giving the order to attack. While they procrastinated, a British fleet stormed into the harbor and demolished the American ships, leaving the survivors to escape on foot back to Boston. Several of the officers were subsequently court-martialed for their parts in the fiasco. One of them was named Paul Revere.

Off Stonington, Deer Isle, sea kayakers' mecca and midpoint of the Maine Island Trail.

WHAT TO EXPECT

Although it traverses some remote areas, the Maine Island Trail should not be considered a wilderness route. If you expect solitude, especially during the high summer months of July and August, you'll be disappointed. But the trail is not an isolated getaway that has become overrun with people—part of the fascination of the Maine coast is its human aspect, from lobster fishermen to historic sailing craft, from old inns to old forts. Allow that fascination to extend to fellow visitors and you'll have a great time. Remember, too, that the Maine Island Trail is also open to small sailboats and even outboard-powered craft.

However, just because there are towns and other boats within view, don't underestimate the ocean here. While it's usually possible to find routes near the mainland coast that are sheltered from the wind, offshore crossings can be exposed. Also, tidal currents in some channels can be very strong (with a tidal range up to 12 feet), and can create confused conditions around river mouths and over shallow bars. The M.I.T.A. guidebook identifies areas where particular caution is needed.

If you do want more solitude, consider coming in September or even October. Weather conditions, especially in October, will be more unsettled and cold, but you'll see far fewer people. April and May are fine, if blustery, but many species of birds are breeding then, and caution is necessary to avoid disturbing them.

Water temperature can vary considerably with location along the coast. One beach might have delightful swimming conditions, while the next will be bone-chilling. Don't expect the water temperature to be over 60°F, and it can still be in the 40s in June. Dress accordingly—thermal stretch should be considered the absolute minimal protection.

Provisioning in Maine is, shall we say, not a problem. Decide you absolutely must have a new sea kayak—at 3:00 A.M.? The L.L. Bean store in Freeport never closes.

1890s hotel, with a justly famous restaurant on the premises. In Deer Isle are two excellent choices, The Inn at Ferry Landing and The Haskell House. On the southern tip of Deer Isle, in Stonington, is The Inn on the Harbor, and near Barred Island Preserve is Goose Cove Lodge. Finally, out on its own on Isle au Haut, is the wonderful Keeper's House, set in an old lighthouse keeper's house.

Maine Island Trail, campsite on an uninhabited island on Muskungus Bay, just south of Penobscot Bay.

GUIDES AND OUTFITTERS

The L.L. Bean Outdoor Discovery School operates numerous excellent programs along the
Maine coast, from introductory kayaking lessons
to 6-day tours. Their parent and child programs
allow kids as young as eight to participate. Maine
Island Kayak Company has similar programs.

L.L. BEAN OUTDOOR DISCOVERY SCHOOL
  Freeport, ME 04033
  800-552-3261
  www.LLBean.com
  $45–$895

MAINE ISLAND KAYAK COMPANY
  70 Luther St.
  Peaks Island, ME 04108
  800-796-2373
  www.maineislandkayak.com
  $55–$875

RECOMMENDED READING

■ *THE MAINE ISLAND TRAIL GUIDEBOOK,*
published annually by the Maine Island Trail
Association (included with membership), is a
must.
■ *MAINE: AN EXPLORER'S GUIDE,* Christina
Tree and Elizabeth Roundy (1999. $18.95. The
Countryman Press.) Very good all-round guide
to the state.

Notre Dame Bay

Front-row paddling on iceberg alley.
Backstage meetings with whales.

B jarni Herjolfsson thought he had it made when he set sail from Iceland in the summer of 985. His *knarr* (longship) was loaded to the gunnels with trade goods for which the luxury-strapped Norse settlers in Greenland would pay handsomely.

But Bjarni and his crew, forced to run downwind before a vicious northeasterly gale in the Denmark Strait, made one of the most fateful detours in history when, after careening south-

west for several days, they found themselves once again in calm water—and within sight of a strange shore, "...not mountainous, but well-wooded and with low hills," as the *Grœnlendinga Saga* tells us. Bjarni didn't land, but sailed up the unfamiliar coast until he figured he was due west of his original goal on Greenland, then left the new world behind. (Bjarni's navigational instincts were uncannily accurate: his landfall on Greenland was within sight of his father's own moored longship.)

Skirting the edge of a "bergy bit," Bay of Exploits.

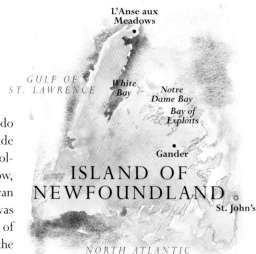

L'Anse aux Meadows

GULF OF ST. LAWRENCE

White Bay

Notre Dame Bay

Bay of Exploits

Gander

ISLAND OF NEWFOUNDLAND

St. John's

NORTH ATLANTIC

Although the sagas do not furnish us with latitude and longitude, most scholars believe that the low, wooded North American shore Bjarni sighted was probably the island of Newfoundland (part of the Province of Newfoundland, which includes Labrador on the mainland). In any case, his tale of the new land fired the imagination of another Viking voyager named Leif Eriksson, and the rest is history: The Vikings founded several settlements in the new world, but eventually abandoned them, leaving Europe in the dark about the existence of America for another 400 years. Perhaps we should be grateful: "Bjarniland the Beautiful" just doesn't have the same ring.

Today you can visit the only Norse settlement yet discovered in North America, at L'Anse aux Meadows on the windy northern tip of the island of Newfoundland, and walk through the reconstructed sod-roofed longhouses. (The Norse built their houses like they built their ships—long and lean.) You can look out over the bay and imagine the dragon-headed longships coming in on the high tide to anchor and off-load the winter's supplies;

vessels manned by some of the finest mariners the world has ever known. It's an inspiring pilgrimage for any small boat pilot.

But, with all due respect to Leif Eriksson et al, the bay at L'Anse aux Meadows is not the best place to sea kayak in Newfoundland. For that you must travel about 150 miles southeast, to a broad, island-filled bay called Notre Dame.

Notre Dame Bay, which is over three times the size of Penobscot Bay in Maine, is set in the crook of a sort of elbow formed by Newfoundland island's northern peninsula. It looks out on a region of the North Atlantic Ocean known as Iceberg Alley because of the hundreds of icebergs that spawn off the Greenland coast, circle Baffin Bay for a year or two, and are then carried by the swift Labrador Current past Labrador and Newfoundland and into the path of big-budget Hollywood movies. In June and July, Notre Dame Bay is like front-row seating for some monstrous parade, as million-ton icebergs float past on the horizon in endless succession. Even better for paddlers, those bergs frequently take tangent courses and wind up grounded in the bay, where they melt in slow, blue-tinged grandeur. Water that has been

AT A GLANCE

TRIP LENGTH 7–10 days
PADDLING DISTANCE 30–100 miles
PHYSICAL CHALLENGE 1 ②③④ 5
MENTAL CHALLENGE 1 ②③④ 5
PRIME TIME June and July

PRICE RANGE (INDEPENDENT TRIP) $650–$950
PRICE RANGE (OUTFITTED GROUP TRIP) $1,200
STAGING CITY St. John's, Newfoundland

Isolated houses connected by boardwalks cling to the weather-beaten shores of Upper Exploits Harbor.

locked away for perhaps millions of years streams off shoulders and cornices on the ice, giving kayakers a frigid shower if they dare paddle underneath. The yearly parade results in the most accessible iceberg viewing in North America.

The Labrador Current brings millions of tons of another blessing to Notre Dame Bay: krill—masses of tiny crustaceans that form the most important food base in the ocean. The krill in turn attract large numbers of whales, especially minke and humpbacks, and several species of seal. The volume of krill carried by the current can be imagined when you know that a single humpback whale can consume two thousand pounds of it— in one day. The summer whale population in Notre Dame is high enough that breathtaking encounters are almost assured. Occasionally orcas can be seen as well.

Iceberg and whale watching are the signature activities in Notre Dame Bay, but this destination would be splendid even without these bonuses. In fact, Notre Dame might have been designed by the patron saint of sea kayakers. The islands scattered throughout the bay (especially in the more sheltered region known as the Bay of Exploits), and the many inlets along the southern coast, provide well-spaced safe landing spots and free primitive campsites. Some of the islands are wilderness; others retain evidence of the fishing families who lived on them until the government of Premier Joseph Smallwood forced them to relocate so government services could be consolidated after World War II. So there's plenty here for both naturalists and amateur anthropologists to investigate. Still, perhaps the best activity of all is simply sitting on a high promontory in the warm summer sun, watching the distant ice, looking for the telltale spouts of whales in the water below—and imagining the boats of long-dead seafarers ghosting between the islands.

In one of the reconstructed longhouses at L'Anse aux Meadows is a *faering,* the small, oared boat used for fishing and shoreline excursions by the Norse (and still to be found working in Norway and the Shetlands). The 10th-century settlers would certainly have ranged into Notre Dame Bay in their quests for fish and meat to put up for Newfoundland's long, cold winters. But the Norse were but one of the many hardy peoples who have braved life on this easternmost outpost of North America. Human history in Newfoundland spans 11,000 years, from the aboriginal hunters who followed the retreat of the great glaciers, to the Maritime Archaic People who occupied the island 3,500 years ago, to the extinct Beothuk Indians who died out completely in 1829, to the modern descendants of European pioneers.

The pilot of a sea kayak, which boasts direct lineage with the earliest aboriginal craft to skirt this shore, has an insight into the spirit of that hardy self-sufficiency unmatched by any other visitor—a kinship that fades into insignificance only in the presence of the ancient icebergs, older than the oldest humans.

SUGGESTED ROUTES

A good launching spot is Lawrence Hole on the Bay of Exploits. From here it's about eight miles to Swan Island, which makes a fine first night's camp. After that the bay is wide open to spontaneous changes of itinerary, due either to weather factors or whims. Other islands within easy day paddle reach include Black, Exploits, and Samson.

All have good beaches for landing—mostly cobble, but some sand—and are suitable for primitive camping. In this part of the bay you are almost always within quick reach of shelter should the wind come up suddenly, as it can at any time of year and from any direction.

The landscape toward the east end of Notre Dame Bay tends to be low and gently sloping, so there are safe put-in spots in sheltered smaller bays, such as the Bay of Exploits. Toward the west end the terrain becomes more abrupt, and there are exposed cliffs up to 150 feet high where on bouncy days the surf flings spray high in the air. It's great fun for experienced paddlers to skirt these cliffs just outside the zone of reflected wave action, or for beginners to stroke right in underneath them on calm days.

Experienced paddlers can explore the more exposed regions of Notre Dame Bay by paddling west out around the port of Fortune into the many inlets in the west part of the bay. If you can arrange a vehicle shuttle it's possible to go as far as White Bay, about 80 miles away, and drive back from Purbeck's Cove. Twenty miles in the other direction is the village of Twillingate, on its own island, with a spectacular view of iceberg alley.

SO YOU THINK VIKING *MEN* WERE TOUGH?

The Vikings mostly reaped what they sowed in their dealings with the tribes they encountered in Newfoundland and Labrador—one of the first exploratory expeditions, led by Thorvald Eriksson, captured eight indigenes and, for no reason that survived telling, killed them all. This act helped spark a war of retribution that was eventually decided in the natives' favor. In the intervening years there were dozens of skirmishes, the outcomes of which swung back and forth with chance and circumstance. But one Viking victory stands out as . . .noteworthy.

A daughter of Erik the Red, Freydis, was part of a two-ship expedition to the new world, a shore party of which was attacked by a much larger force of *Skraelings*. The Viking men broke ranks and ran for cover under a hail of arrows, but Freydis, who was pregnant, could not keep up with them. So she plucked a broadsword from the body of a companion and turned to face the attacking mob. Ripping open her bodice, she exposed her breasts and began beating them with the flat of the sword while advancing on the astonished natives, who stopped in their tracks, stared at the awful apparition, and then fled in abject terror.

One can only imagine what Freydis had to say to the burly warriors picking arrows out of their backsides back at the ship.

Melting Newfoundland iceberg. This ice is estimated to be some 10,000 years old.

also many provincial parks for those who prefer organized camping facilities. As for the people, Newfoundlanders are extremely friendly, but you might have to make the first move to open a conversation, and the broad accent of many takes some getting used to.

Although Notre Dame Bay (including the Bay of Exploits) offers routes that take advantage of the sheltering islands and bays, this is still not a destination for an unescorted novice. Not only are water temperatures very cold (all those melting bergs render the place one big iced drink), but the region is susceptible to thick fog that makes navigation difficult, as well as sudden summer storms that rough up even sheltered water. But to paddlers with proper experience and safety skills, such factors only add to the appeal.

A full wet suit is the minimum outerwear for Notre Dame Bay, and a dry suit is better. Be prepared for sudden shifts from clear to stormy conditions, and plan all crossings carefully—even those of only a couple of miles. Tides are not much of a factor in the bay; the range is only about six feet and currents are mostly slow. Fog can roll in at any time, however, so watch for the telltale low gray bank approaching from either the land or sea. If you find yourself near a pub, try the traditional Newfoundland cure for hypothermia, a serious rum called Screech.

What to Expect

St. John's, where most flights come into Newfoundland, is some 200 miles from Notre Dame Bay. Local connecting flights access Gander, which is much closer (within 25 miles) and serves well as a regional base.

Accommodations on Newfoundland range from adequate hotels and motels in major towns (St. John's, Deer Lake, Gander) to bed-and-breakfast establishments (known as hospitality homes here) in outlying areas. There are

Guides and Outfitters

OUTSIDE EXPEDITIONS
P.O. Box 337
North Rustico PEI, C0A 1X0 Canada
800-207-3899
www.adventuresports.com
$1,295 for 7 days (Notre Dame Bay and other areas)

GROS MORNE ADVENTURE GUIDES
Norris Point, NF, A0K 3Y0 Canada
800-685-4624
www.grosmorneadventures.com
$1,295 for 8 days (Notre Dame Bay)

A cobble cove on Upper Black Island, perfect place to beach the boats and take a stretch.

RECOMMENDED READING

■ *THE BOAT WHO WOULDN'T FLOAT,* Farley Mowat (1984. $4.99. Banatm Books.) A zany account of the author's misadventures with a sailboat off the Atlantic coast of Canada.

■ *THE SHIPPING NEWS,* E. Annie Proulx (1993. $12.00. Simon and Schuster.) A luminous, Pulitzer Prize-winning story of life and love in Newfoundland.

CANADA'S NEWEST PROVINCE

Newfoundland was an independent colony of the Crown until 1948, when by a thin 2 percent margin the residents voted to, as they would have you believe, allow Canada to join them. The pre-war years had been hard, especially in the 1930s when the economy, which was then almost solely dependent on fishing, collapsed. After the war it was time for a change, and Newfoundland's first premier, Joseph Smallwood, engineered just that, broadening the economic base to include logging and mining, and wooing corporations with financial incentives.

The province honors Smallwood's administration with somewhat mixed feelings—although many of his programs failed, and he was responsible for the relocation of many families, he nevertheless revitalized Newfoundland as an economic force.

Despite the enormous problems presented by the decline of the Grand Banks fish stocks, fishing continues to be an important part of Newfoundland's economy, along with paper and pulp production, mining, and, increasingly, tourism.

Daytrips

Cape Town, South Africa

he view from the boisterous waters of Table Bay, over the beautiful Victoria and Alfred Waterfront and the skyline of Cape Town, and up the green slopes of Table Mountain to the clouds rolling over its summit, must be one of the most magnificent cityscapes in the world. Despite its growing pains (like any large city in the world, there are parts of Cape Town through which you should avoid carrying your kayak), the gateway to southern Africa makes a gracious stopover at the end of a trip in the bush.

The Victoria and Alfred Waterfront is named for Queen Victoria and her second son, Alfred, who tipped the first load of stone to begin construction of the Cape Town breakwater in 1860. There are two harbor basins now, ringed with luxurious hotels such as the Table Bay Hotel and the splendid Cape Grace, worth splurging on for a night or two. The waterfront shopping complex, while bordering on kitsch, never seems to quite go over the edge, and there are several truly superior shops, especially for jewelry.

The Victoria and Alfred Basins were certainly not designed for kayakers, but they're great to poke around in nonetheless. You can't launch in the basins, but must come around the breakwater from Granger Bay, to the west. This exposes you to the full effects of the South Atlantic Ocean, so choose your weather carefully.

In the basins you'll spot cantankerous cape fur seals, which have appropriated docks here just as other seals do in other harbors worldwide. You'll also see some yachts of mind-boggling dimensions tied up to quays, while their owners are ashore buying diamonds or something. If you like, you can also head east of the Victoria and Alfred Area, to the much larger commercial docks past South Arm breakwater. Past them is Big Bay, a famous beach and windsurfing area. You can land there, but the surf is often high. The water off Cape Town is also very cold; make sure you wear immersion protection if you go.

Paddling distance is approximately 3 to 5 miles.

Above: Cape Town from Table Mountain. Cape Town is at the northwestern base of the Cape of Good Hope.
Opposite: The Cape of Good Hope and the vast South Atlantic; Antarctica, the nearest land, is 2,500 miles south.

Baja California

Desert against ocean—
the most striking coastline in the world.

It was a clear and warm, but windy, late afternoon on the Sea of Cortéz, and our party of six was sheltered in the lee of a cliff just above high tide line, on a rocky point about 20 miles south of Bahia de los Angeles, Baja California Norte. We sat on boulders, Pacifico beers in hand, chatting and gazing east over the water as whitecaps rolled by on their way south. Suddenly someone shouted "Dolphins!" We looked to see a pod of 10 or so common dolphins

racing north against the waves, occasionally leaping clear of the water. It was a sight we never tired of, although this time I thought I noticed an extra urgency to the dolphins' rush.

The reason became clear no more than two minutes later, when someone else shouted "Orcas!" I looked out again and saw five or six of the distinctive black and white shapes plunging along in the wake of the dolphins. Orcas are resident in the Sea of Cortéz, but rarely seen, and to

Heading toward Bahia de los Angeles, an island-dotted bay one-third of the way down Baja Peninsula.

San Diego • UNITED STATES

MEXICO

ISLA ANGEL DE
LA GUARDA
Bahia de los Angeles •
ISLA TIBURON

SAN LORENZO
SAN ESTEBAN

BAJA

SEA OF CORTÉZ

• La Paz

spot these in an apparent life-and-death race with a group of dolphins was thrilling and eerily chilling. It was impossible not to hope that the dolphins would escape, just this once. The six of us scrambled to the top of the cliff and watched through our binoculars until the white flashes of the orcas diminished to a vanishing point. Moments later the sun winked out behind the desert hills as if a curtain had been drawn over the drama, its denouement forever unknown. I retired that night with my heart full of the heady mixture of exhilaration and poignancy that is like a drug to the true naturalist; the whirlwind of emotions elicited by the stoop of a falcon on a partridge, or the leap of a tiger on a stag.

Asked to name the most beautiful seascape in the world, I would wince, whine, and demur. Not possible, I'd say; it would be sacrilegious to pick one above all others, when there are so many exquisite possibilities. The twenty most beautiful, certainly. Ten, perhaps. One? Not a chance.

Yet, if intimidated into nominating but a single choice—say, by a large man holding an ax and threatening to force-feed me okra—I would unhesitatingly pick the Sea of Cortéz and its Sonoran Desert coast. And an informal poll among four better-traveled-than-I paddling acquaintances produced the same response from no fewer than three of them.

I can already hear the cries of outrage. What about the Pacific Northwest? The north coast of Scotland? Tierra del Fuego? Sublime choices, all. But the juxtaposition of a desert and an ocean adds a dimension of contrast unmatched by any other meeting of land and sea, a piquancy that sharpens the senses, clarifying line and deepening color. And the Sonoran Desert is certainly the most beautiful desert on earth, with its ascetic but unexpectedly lush flora of columnar cacti, thorned shrubs, and spined trees. Here is the ultimate paradox: a world of infinite water set against a world of unforgiving aridity. The sea kayaker who flirts with the edge of these worlds bridges a narrow line dividing the two most disparate environments on earth.

The Baja California peninsula was part of mainland North America until about 12 million

Overleaf: Sand dunes on Bahia Magdalena, three-quarters of the way down the west coast of Baja.

AT A GLANCE

TRIP LENGTH 3–7 days
PADDLING DISTANCE 10–40 miles
PHYSICAL CHALLENGE   1 ②③ 4 5
MENTAL CHALLENGE ①② 3 4 5
PRIME TIME December–April. Avoid Christmas and Easter, the only times the bay gets really crowded.

PRICE RANGE (INDEPENDENT TRIP) $240–$400
PRICE RANGE (OUTFITTED GROUP TRIP) $425–$500
STAGING CITY San Diego, California
HEADS UP The wind here is often underestimated

Rock formations at the southern tip of the peninsula, where the Sea of Cortéz and the Pacific meet.

years ago, when the block faulting and subsidence that formed much of the southwestern United States topography allowed a long finger of the Pacific Ocean to wash its way north, well into what is now Arizona and California. Later, beginning around 5 million years ago, the same fault system that also sporadically attempts to make the state of California a peninsula further spread and deepened the gulf. Meanwhile sedimentation from the Colorado River basin filled in the northern part, forming the Imperial Valley.

The result of all this tectonic ditch-digging was the Sea of Cortéz (also called the Gulf of California), one of the most biologically diverse seas in the world. Nearly 700 miles long (span-

ning nine degrees of latitude), surrounded on three sides by land, and with an opening to the Pacific less than 200 miles wide, much of it functions effectively as a closed ecosystem, resulting in an extremely high percentage of endemic species (those that evolved there). Only half of the estimated 10,000 invertebrate species in the gulf have even been described.

The Sonoran Desert, which covers much of Baja and the mainland coast (as well as southern Arizona), is considerably younger than the sea it borders, developing mostly after the end of the last ice age just 10,000 to 12,000 years ago. Many of the signature plants of the desert, especially the columnar cacti such as saguaros, organ pipes, and *cardóns* (see box below), evolved in tropical Mexico farther south, and slowly migrated north with the increase in temperatures.

This landscape is a servant to its rainfall, from under four inches a year in spots to around ten (at times I've felt I had that much dropped on me during *lunch* in Washington State). But desert plants make the most of it: In January vast areas of the desert are carpeted in wildflowers nourished by December showers; oranges, yellows, purples, and crimsons in overpowering profusion. Winter and early spring months are, fortuitously, the best for paddling here: Daytime temperatures hover in the 70s; nights rarely drop below 45°F, and the occasional, colder rainstorms are welcomed as the visitor can witness their effects on shrubs and grasses within hours.

The crown jewels of the Sea of Cortéz are 35 major islands and dozens of smaller islets scattered along its length. These islands rival the Galapagos in their importance as natural laboratories for evolutionary biology, and nearly all retain intact a majority of their original ecosystems. Even Isla Tiburon, at nearly 400 square miles the largest in the gulf, has never been grazed by domesticated animals. The isolation of the islands has resulted in a degree of endemism among their terrestrial organisms at least as great as in the surrounding

Top: Exploring islets in the Sea of Cortéz. Above: The Sierra de la Garganta range drops dramatically down to the east coast south of Loreto.

BIG CACTUS

Towering over the desert scrub in Bahia de los Angeles are giant columnar cacti that look like the saguaros of so many western postcards. But these are different. Called *cardóns* (*Pachycereus pringlei*), they don't grow as tall as saguaros—topping out at 35 feet or so—but are more massive, often weighing over ten tons.

The *cardón* photosynthesizes through the thick, waxy green skin of its succulent trunk and arms, so it doesn't need leaves (which would waste too much

water through evaporation). The waxy skin further slows dessication, and the limbs store enormous amounts of water that the plant can use during prolonged droughts. *Cardóns* grow slowly, and, while difficult to date (since they have no growth rings like a tree), are thought to reach ages of 250 to 300 years.

The Native Americans of Baja and the Mexican mainland ate the fruit of *cardóns* and used the long woody ribs of dead ones in house construction.

waters. Fully half of the 120 species of cacti found on the islands evolved there, as well as an entire genus of lizard (*Sator*), and 15 species of mammals. There are peculiar individual conundrums of evolution to intrigue the naturalist: a species of rattlesnake on one island that has lost its rattle, a jackrabbit with pale fur on another that stands out starkly on its volcanic home.

When the cold winds of winter sweep in across the Pacific Northwest and the "Down East" coast of Maine, the warm sun of the Sea of Cortéz is a powerful siren call to northern paddlers. There are dozens of paddling routes here, the vast majority of them along the Baja coast (although the mainland coast north of Guaymas is just as superb). Most kayakers, and most tour operators, base their trips in southern Baja, around La Paz and Loreto, both of which can be reached quickly by air from the United States.

For serious naturalists, however, the pinnacle of the Sea of Cortéz experience might be had in Bahia de los Angeles, an enormous, island-dotted bay about one-third of the way down the peninsula, a long day's drive (about 400 miles) from San Diego. There is a small community here, with several restaurants, campgrounds, a Pemex gas station, and even an excellent, if humble, natural history museum. However, the town's electricity is still provided by generator, so it's lights out at 10:00 P.M. In spite of being closer to the United States than the towns farther south, there are fewer tourists and fewer paddlers, making it

BIG LIZARDS

The first sight of one is enough to send any non-herpetologist running for the nearest tree—if there were any trees big enough to climb. Chuckwallas (*Sauromalus obesus*) can reach a foot and a half in length and weigh upwards of two pounds. Their size, combined with their generally belligerent appearance, keeps most humans at bay.

But chuckwallas, it turns out, are strict vegetarians, dining on fruits, leaves, and flowers of desert plants (which isn't to say they can't give you a painful chomp if you decide to wrestle with one).

They emerge from rock crevices when the sun comes up, bask until their body temperature reaches 100 degrees or so, and then begin foraging. If pursued—by humans, raptors, or coyotes—they'll dive back into a crevice and inflate their bodies until they stick tight, almost immune to prying loose.

Chuckwallas can be found on the mainland of Baja, and on several of the islands in Bahia de los Angeles. Endemic species live on Isla Angel de la Guarda and Isla San Esteban.

Boats at Punta Pescador. Isla Angel de la Guarda is in the background.

much easier to experience the solitude that should accompany warm desert nights under the stars.

Bahia de los Angeles stands out even in this fertile sea because of the deep trenches that plunge to 2,000 feet or more in the channel between the bay and the big island of Angel de la Guarda, about 10 miles offshore. The cold water in these trenches is densely oxygenated and richly productive, and constant upwelling from the deep water moves tons of plankton into the shallower waters of the bay. As a result, Bahia de los Angeles boasts a large and diverse population of marine mammals, including a dozen species of whale such as blue, finback, gray, pilot, and humpback, as well as dolphins and sea lions. The baleen whales feed

directly on the plankton, while the toothed whales feed on vast numbers of fish that are themselves plankton feeders. Thousands of seabirds are also supported by this abundance, and you're likely to spot exceptionally fat coyotes beachcombing for carrion.

My favorite activity in Bahia de los Angeles is catching finback whales. Well, not really catching, but here's what you do. Fin whales are peculiar in that the right side of their lower jaw is white, while the left is dark. They are also peculiar in that they normally feed in a clockwise circle. It's thought that the white spot startles the shoals of plankton and tiny fish on which the whales prey, and that they actually herd their prey into smaller

On a seven-day tour around Isla Espiritu Sano near La Paz, among the most popular kayaking waters.

and smaller circles until they can grab an enormous mouthful. If you sit in your kayak on a quiet day and watch a fin whale feeding, you can sometimes predict roughly where it will surface for its next breath, and paddle to the general area and wait quietly. Just occasionally, the trick works perfectly, and a 70-foot-long whale will surface with a mighty exhalation close enough to make you feel very, very small.

It's another one of those naturalist rushes.

SUGGESTED ROUTES

Fifteen small islands within the perimeter of Bahia de los Angeles are all accessible within a few hours of paddling. Most have at least one beach of sand or gravel suitable for landing and camping. Heading out of the bay and south along the coast for ten miles will bring you to the remote and lovely Bahia las Animas (Bay of Souls), which has miles of gentle sand beaches for landing and camping. From here, adventur-

ous, and *very* experienced, paddlers can actually cross the Sea of Cortéz to the mainland, using the midriff islands of San Lorenzo, San Esteban, and Tiburon as stepping-stones. I've tried this route twice, and both times I wound up stormed in on San Esteban, eventually running out of time and retreating. Someday. . .

The nearest islands, Ventana and Cabeza de Caballo, are about three and four miles offshore, respectively. If you want to head south from Bahia de los Angeles to Bahia las Animas, there is a protected inlet called Puerto Don Juan at the far eastern arm of Bahia de los Angeles, which offers a sheltered stopover if the wind picks up.

WHAT TO EXPECT

The people of Baja are used to tourists, and it's nearly always possible to find someone who speaks English. The farther you get from major tourist towns, the friendlier the people. At this time no visa is needed for travel in Baja; however, check with the Mexican Consulate before you go. Buy all your supplies in San Diego; a few basic groceries are available in the village of Bahia de los Angeles

Guillermo's Restaurant is on the beach in the middle of the town of Bahia de los Angeles, and offers camping and long-term parking for a fee.

The arbiter of paddling in Bahia de los Angeles is the wind, which has caught many inexperienced *and* experienced paddlers off guard here. Normally mornings are calm, afternoons breezy or windy. But frequent winter winds known as "Northers" or "El Norte" can come up suddenly and blow 20 to 30 knots for days on end. Waves within the bay are generally not very big, due to the short fetch; nevertheless caution is mandatory. The water temperature is colder than you might expect (below 60°F in places), because of the upwelling from deep channels, so some form of protective clothing such as thermal stretch is needed for immersion insulation. Prevailing winter winds, including the Northers, originate from the north or northwest, but can change unexpectedly. Even for day paddles to the inner islands it is wise to be prepared for an overnight stay or two (I know someone with a 27-foot diesel cabin cruiser who was stranded on Angel de la Guarda for several days by weather). Carry one gallon of water per person per day.

The tidal range in the midriff area of the Sea of Cortéz is not great, but currents can be very fast, especially off points and between islands. Carry a tidal chart.

There are dozens of wilderness camping spots on the islands and mainland coast. Some of the beaches on islands nearest the town can be littered with fish carcasses and garbage from fishermen; the farther away you get, the smaller this problem becomes.

There are rattlesnakes and scorpions on the mainland of Baja, and on many of the islands as well. The danger from rattlesnake bite has been grossly overexaggerated, as bites are rare and fatal-

ities from them even more so. Nevertheless, when you are hundreds of miles from medical help caution is advisable to avoid both rattlesnakes and scorpions (the latter often crawl under tents at night). Watch where you walk and put your hands. Do not walk around at night without shoes or a flashlight. If you are lucky enough to see a rattlesnake, simply leave it alone. A scorpion sting will cause you several hours of significant pain, but nothing else unless you suffer an allergic reaction.

GUIDES AND OUTFITTERS

Southwest Sea Kayaks in San Diego runs many trips to Bahia de los Angeles, mostly of the self-catering sort: you bring and cook your own food. They're very reasonable and include a discount if you have your own kayak. Paddling South operates fully catered and equipped tours in the Loreto area.

SOUTHWEST SEA KAYAKS

2590 Ingraham St.
San Diego, CA 92109
619-222-3616
www.swkayaks.com
$425 for 5 days

PADDLING SOUTH

4510 Silverado Trail
Calistoga, CA 94515
707-942-4550
$995 for 9 days

RECOMMENDED READING

■ *SEA KAYAKING IN BAJA,* Andromeda Romano-Lax (1993. $13.95. Wilderness Press.) An excellent guide for paddlers; includes several recommended routes.

■ *THE VERMILLION SEA,* John Janovy, Jr (1992. Houghton Mifflin.) A naturalist's musings on Baja. A splendid introduction to the ecology of the Sea of Cortéz and Baja. Out of print, but worth searching for.

Lofoten Islands

A dramatic seascape churned by Viking longships and maelstroms.

Two magnificent, overwhelming pres-
ences vie for dominance in the
Norwegian landscape: the ocean and the
mountains.

Each seems to perpetually challenge the
other, an irresistible force in oft-broken armistice
with an immovable object. The mountains rise
abruptly, massively, and solidly from the abyssal
waters, with rarely such an ephemeral juncture as
might be called a shore—*breastworks* would be a

more apt term. And the ocean continually tests
those defenses, both by the direct assault of
storms pounding against the outer coast, and by
the subterfuge of the fjords probing dozens of
miles inland like flanking maneuvers.

But it's not all a contest of force and resistance. The land and sea strive to outdo each
other in majesty as well. The Norwegian Sea has
the elemental beauty of oceans everywhere,
compounded by the power and color imbued by

Campsite on a small island off the northwest coast of the Lofoten Island chain.

ATLANTIC

SWEDEN

LOFOTEN ISLANDS

OSTVAAGØY
VESTAAGØY
FLAKSTADØY
MOSKENESØY

• Bodo

NORWEGIAN
SEA

NORWAY

tempestuous northern latitudes. It snaps back and forth in mercurial moods between deep blue and even deeper black.

The mountains, for all their immutable strength, cloak themselves in finery of the most delicate cloth. Everything that is not bare rock is green—a rich pine and heather and lichen green, punctuated on every slope by thin white veils of waterfalls, braided lace on emerald baize. When the ocean rages, the mountains and their valleys soothe and shelter.

Viewing this dramatic coastline, it seems self-evident that such a land would produce a nation of seafarers and a tradition of sturdy, capable ships—and it has, perhaps the finest sailors and boats the world has ever known, from the Vikings and their longships to the 19th-century fishermen and polar explorers in stout, double-ended sailing craft, and the even stouter *Redningskoite* rescue ketches capable of clawing their way offshore through any storm. And there was Fritjof Nansen's *Fram,* which got closer to the North Pole than any sailing craft before or since. The *Fram* had an oak hull three feet thick at the bow to fend off ice (you can explore the ship today in Oslo). Even today, a Norwegian-built ship or any ship boasting a Norwegian captain is accorded an extra measure of respect and confidence anywhere in the world.

Given this heady maritime tradition, it's surprising to note that modern sea kayaking had a slow start in Norway. Perhaps it is because the Norwegians still tend to view boats as tools, or because of a vague atavistic sense that a 17-foot-long boat should weigh at least a ton or two if it is to be considered seaworthy! Whatever the reasons, the sea kayak is now enjoying a surge of popularity—organized sea kayaking clubs are becoming common, often boasting group facilities and boat storage for members. This enthusiastic swell is fitting for a country that seems to have been designed with sea kayaking in mind.

Norway is long and narrow—pivot the country around its southern tip and the north cape would swipe Venice. Along the coast, 900 miles long in a straight line, hundreds of fjords provide shelter from the open sea (although many are big enough to have their own weather) as well as awe-inspiring vistas from the waterline.

AT A GLANCE

TRIP LENGTH 3–10 days
PADDLING DISTANCE 60–120 miles
PHYSICAL CHALLENGE 1 ②③④ 5
MENTAL CHALLENGE 1 2 ③ 4 5
PRIME TIME May–August (April and September for fewer people and rougher weather)

PRICE RANGE (INDEPENDENT TRIP) $450–$1,200
PRICE RANGE (OUTFITTED GROUP TRIP)
$50–$1,650
STAGING CITY Svolvaer, Norway

Near the historic Tinden Trading Post on Tinsøy Island just north of the Lofoten chain.

Norway has the lowest population density of any country in mainland Europe; a third of its land and half its coast lies above the Arctic Circle. The result is miles and miles of uninhabited green ramparts rising giddily above a paddler's head, with the occasional relief of a glade sloping gently to the water's edge, often as not scattered with a few tidy, colorful wood houses, like some cheery refuge in an epic seagoing fantasy.

About 100 miles north of the Arctic Circle, one of the most striking archipelagoes in the world defies the Norwegian Sea. Thrusting west and south in a ragged, curving chain, the steep mountain ramparts of the Lofoten Islands—jagged, permanently snowcapped peaks up to 4,000 feet high—block the fiercest of the Arctic winter gales that sweep in from the northwest. Exploiting this natural windbreak, fishing villages huddle cozily beside coves and fjords in the lee of the peaks, looking out over the bay of Vestfjorden toward the mainland.

The Lofotens comprise four main islands (connected by road and bridge) and hundreds of smaller ones. There is a surprisingly large population here, about 25,000, but it's mostly clustered in villages or small hamlets on bays and fjords. Fishing is still the major occupation, down only slightly from the heyday of small-boat cod fishing 50 years ago, when 6,000 boats a day ventured out of the Lofotens in late winter.

In addition to their dramatic backdrop and edge-of-the-world Arctic location, the Lofotens have several characteristics that make this a superb paddling area. First, while there are enough villages that you could paddle from one to the next and never need to sleep outdoors, there are also enough deserted and, astonishingly, sandy beaches that you could camp your way along the chain in happy solitude. Second, while you must be constantly aware of tidal currents in the fjords and interisland channels, and on the lookout for the occasional southeasterly fronts, in general the paddling here is sheltered from the brunt of North Sea weather. Finally, despite the Arctic location, access to the Lofotens is straightforward, either by car or coastal ferry.

Ten days in the Lofoten Islands can produce a store of memories equivalent to those from a month spent in many more ordinary destinations. There is the constant sweep of scenery, the busy harbors infused with the noises of people and boats working the sea, the bright villages smelling of fish pudding and sweet pastries, and a realization of history that plunges back beyond the Vikings, beyond the Stone Age fishermen casting bone hooks into the fjords, back to the very origins of the world. For much of the rock that forms the spine of the archipelago was born of volcanic forges billions of years ago, and comprises some of the oldest exposed formations on earth. Look up at the mountains and you are peeking at ingots cooled straight from the anvil of Odin (the supreme being in Norse mythology).

In the end, though, as a kayaker you're most likely to have your blood stirred by the last few centuries of activity around the Lofotens: the heady traditions of seamanship that began with the Vikings and continues with their descendants. A sea kayaker who has explored the coasts and fjords of Norway can rightfully claim a link to that bold legacy. While I wouldn't suggest adopting a horned helmet, you might visit the restored chieftain's longhouse at the Viking museum in Borg, on Vestaagøy, after you've unpacked your kayak at the end of the trip. It'll be effortless to imagine yourself drinking mead

Above: The village of Hamnoy on the island of Moskenesøy, just south of the Moskenstraumen Maelstrom

THOSE COLORFUL BUILDINGS

The brilliant palette of so many Norwegian settlements has its origins not in aesthetic preferences, but in thrift. It used to be that red was the cheapest paint to buy, so that was what the poorest owners used. Blues, yellows, and greens cost more, and thus marked increasingly affluent neighborhoods. And, oddly, the most expensive and least durable color of all was white, so a plain white house was considered a mark of ultimate status. Paint eventually became standardized, but by then those bright colors had become second nature.

and chewing on a giant joint of beef, debating which country to sack next.

SUGGESTED ROUTES

The beauty of archipelagoes such as the Lofotens is that there are no standard paths to be overrun by crowds. You'll have a choice of dozens of possible itineraries. However, unless you are an expert paddler, plan to stay on the sheltered, inland side of the islands.

From Svolvaer a couple of major options beckon.

You can paddle southwest along the islands, hopping from Ostvaagøy to Vestaagøy, Flakstadøy, and finally to Moskenesøy, ending in the small and briefly named town of Å (which is the last letter in the Norwegian alphabet). You will want to quit in Å, because just off the southern tip of Moskenesøy is the Moskenstraumen Maelstrom, through which you do not wish to paddle (see box below).

The other option is to head east, to the small island of Store Molla, then into the Raftsundet channel to explore the delightfully named Trollfjord, which slices deeply inland between the mountains. An even more remote fjord, Øksfjord, farther east, has a hiking trail near its end that climbs into the ancient ice-crusted granite peaks.

Although no strait between the individual Lofoten Islands is wider than a mile or two at the narrowest spot, the channels funnel wind from the north, and can be swept by fast tidal currents, so take care with crossings. Tidal charts are available, which help you to time cycles, but ask locally about conditions—you'll always get better information.

Opposite: Approaching a sea cave on the north coast of Lofoten Island, northernmost of the Lofoten islands. Accessible only by small boat, it contains Bronze Age cave drawings.

THE MAELSTROMS

Norway is famous for two of the most violent ocean phenomena in the world.

One is just off the western end of the Lofoten Islands. Called the Moskenstraumen Maelstrom (or Malstrøm), it is created by a shallow bench in the sea floor over which the tidal flow surges, spawning large whirlpools described with dramatic effect by such writers as Jules Verne and Edgar Allen Poe. Renowned as a boat killer (with some justification), the maelstrom is actually looked on by local fishermen with some fondness, since the roiling water contains massive shoals of herring.

A much more visually impressive maelstrom occurs just south of the mainland town of Bodø in a large fjord called Skerstad, where the incoming and outgoing tides are forced through a channel only 500 feet wide. Four times each day over 500 million cubic yards of seawater surges through this chute, creating an apocalyptic overfall of churning waves and vast whirlpools known as the Saltstraumen Maelstrom. It is the most powerful tidal current in the world, and the fastest at up to a staggering 20 knots (23 mph). Even the noise it produces is chilling. Unlike the famous Corryvreckan off Scotland, which is regularly challenged by expert kayakers, *nothing* goes through the Saltstraumen at the height of its fury. During World War II a German warship in pursuit of resistance fighters was lured into the strait as the maelstrom raged full force. The ship broke in two.

So—while they're not to be considered a paddling destination, the maelstroms are certainly worth experiencing from the safety of shore.

The terrain for launchings and landings varies from sheer escarpments to surprisingly gentle sand beaches in sheltered coves. You can count on virtually any coastal village to have a protected harbor.

WHAT TO EXPECT

Getting around in Norway is easy and fast, thanks to an excellent road and coastal ferry network. It's always possible to find someone who speaks fluent English. But things aren't all rosy: Liquor of all types is strictly regulated in Norway, and prices are steep enough to dry out the hardest-drinking group of kayakers.

The most beautiful way to get to the Lofotens is by driving up Norway's stunning coastal road Number 17, which crosses a number of fjords by ferry (on one of these you'll cross the Arctic Circle as well), ending in Bodø and a ferry to Svolvaer. The alternate is the inland route, E6, which goes all the way to the islands. There is also air service to Svolvaer from Bodø.

Svolvaer, the main town of the Lofotens, on the island of Ostvaagøy, has hotels, restaurants, and grocery stores, but no kayaking equipment. Bring your own gear.

The most rewarding tours of the Lofotens combine wilderness and civilization, since it would be a shame to shun the friendliness of the Norwegian people (to make friends in Norway, just stand on a street corner with an open map and a puzzled expression). You can orient yourself in Svolvaer while staying in one of over a half-dozen hotels, or in the decidedly more romantic (and less costly) surroundings of a *rorbu,* a unique Lofoten relic.

In about A.D. 1120 King Øystein built a series of cabins in the Lofotens, as accommodations for fishermen staying there through the harsh winter cod season. The cabins, called *rorbuen,* multiplied with the fishery and were soon in every village on the islands. With the decline of the industry most of the *rorbuen* fell into disuse—until someone got the idea to convert them into inexpensive hotels for travelers. Now anyone can rent one; a *rorbu* contains beds and hot showers and sometimes laundry facilities. There is at least one in every sizable village in the Lofotens.

If you'd like a fairly luxurious base for your tour, try the Rica Hotel Svolvaer, a waterfront establishment modeled after the *rorbuen,* but quite a bit more upscale inside.

Camping is allowed on any deserted shoreline in the Lofotens. If you are within sight of a farmhouse or other habitation you should ask permission first. Organized campgrounds are common everywhere in Norway. Most of them are equipped with wood huts, but you can pitch a tent if you prefer.

The Lofotens are gaining just a bit of well-deserved repute as a sea kayaking destination. If you prefer to do your paddling completely alone, come at the edges of the summer season, when

Above: The many small, rocky islets of the Lofotens make ideal rookeries for gulls and other seabirds.

the weather is more unsettled. You'll still have enough good days to paddle.

Although the Lofoten Islands are on the same latitude as Inuvik in the Northwest Territories, the warming effect of the Gulf Stream results in milder weather conditions. With that said, fierce storms can still strike at any time of year, and travelers should be prepared for cold and wet. Although the prevailing summer winds are blocked by the mountains, occasional fronts can reverse things, sending heavy surf on to normally protected shores. Check local weather reports, which sometimes predict such cycles. The water around the Lofotens is comparatively warm thanks to the Gulf Stream, but it rarely reaches 60°F in the summer. Wear proper protective clothing, either thermal stretch or neoprene, while paddling.

GUIDES AND OUTFITTERS

Crossing Latitudes offers an eight-day trip in the Lofotens. Jann's Adventure Lofotens runs trips from several hours to several days in length.

CROSSING LATITUDES

800-572-8747
www.crossinglatitudes.com
$1,650 for 8 days

JANN'S ADVENTURE LOFOTENS

P.O. Box 136
N-8309 Kabelvag, Norway
47-760-78910
www.lofoten-aktiv.no

RECOMMENDED READING

■ *TOPSAIL & BATTLEAXE, A VOYAGE IN THE WAKE OF THE VIKINGS,* Tom Cunliffe (1988. $17.95. David & Charles, London.) An informative and hilarious account of a voyage in an 80-year-old pilot cutter.
■ *NORWAY, THE ROUGH GUIDE,* Jules Brown (2000. $17.95. The Rough Guides.) Just updated. Good information for the independent traveler.

Top: Tim Conlan, a guide with Crossing Latitudes, shows his group the route. Above: Reindeer on a beach where kayakers regularly camp.

Marlborough Sounds & Fiordland National Park

Retracing the routes of Maori war canoes and English brigantines.

I've given myself a challenge. I'm going to convince you that you need to go sea kayaking in New Zealand—and I am going to do it in just two sentences. Ready? Here they are:

1. New Zealand has a longer coastline than the mainland United States.

2. New Zealand has one-fiftieth the population of the United States.

Convinced? I thought so. Now I'll just fill in a few details.

The first time you leaf through a glossy coffee-table book about New Zealand, you might suspect that some incompetent printer had mistakenly placed photographs from eight or nine different countries in there. Here's a double spread showing a forbidding, glaciered range of peaks that could only be the Himalayas. Turn the page to see a whitewashed farmhouse overlooking a pasture filled with contented sheep, apparently a scene from Ireland. Flip to

The Champagne Pool, Waiotapu Thermal area near Rotorua, North Island, New Zealand.

NEW
ZEALAND
Auckland

NORTH ISLAND

TASMAN
SEA
D'URVILLE
ISLAND
Picton   Wellington
Marlborough
Sounds
PACIFIC
Mount Cook
SOUTH ISLAND

Fiordland   Te Anau
National   Manapouri
Park

the next page, which shows a tropi-cal shore lined with palm trees—Tahiti?—and the next, a sea-level view of spectacular Norwegian fjords. Flip: A Tyrolean village nestles between an alpine lake and pine-forested hills. Flip: A geyser shoots sky-ward in Yellowstone. Flip: Yikes. A line of very large men wearing grass skirts and face paint gestures menacingly at the camera.

New Zealand's staggering diversity is no printer's error. Instead, it's the result of a fortu-itous farrago of geographic and anthropologic factors.

Stretched out on a more or less north/south axis, New Zealand's two main islands (called—memorize this carefully—North Island and South Island) span nearly 15 degrees of Southern Hemisphere latitude; if you flopped them onto the United States they would cover Dallas, Texas, and Fargo, North Dakota. Thus, while the south-ern tip of South Island boasts majestic, cold-water fjords overlooking the roaring forties of the Southern Ocean, the northern end of North Island basks in Fiji-esque warmth. In the interior

of South Island, a range of peaks known as the Southern Alps rises to the permanently snowcapped high point of Mount Cook at 12,350 feet. Just to keep things interesting, the continu-ously motile nature of the continental ates underlying New Zealand induces vigorous volcanic activity, including local eruptions and scattered thermal vents and hot springs.

Laid out across this varied landscape is the warp and weft of two cultures that could hardly boast more different origins: the Maori, a Polynesian people whose ancestors colonized North Island about a thousand years ago, and the English, who introduced sheep, cricket, and whitewash during the 19th century. And yet, more so than in many other South Pacific coun-tries, the two groups seem to have arrived at a mutually respectful state of coexistence (although various Maori land claims continue to filter through the courts). The result for the visitor is an engaging mix of European charm and Polynesian joie de vivre.

Since New Zealand's diversity is most exem-plified along its coast, it's nearly impossible to grant exclusivity to a single area as a sea kayaking

AT A GLANCE

TRIP LENGTH 1–2 weeks
PADDLING DISTANCE Highly variable.
A circumnavigation of the Marlborough
Sounds area is about 60 miles.
PHYSICAL CHALLENGE ① ② ③ ④ 5
MENTAL CHALLENGE ① ② ③ 4 5
PRIME TIME November–April

PRICE RANGE (INDEPENDENT TRIP) $275–$675
PRICE RANGE (OUTFITTED GROUP TRIP)
$225– $700
STAGING CITY Auckland, New Zealand

Marlborough Sounds, the sheltered waters where Captain Cook anchored Endeavor *during his first journey to New Zealand.*

destination. From a solid half-dozen candidates, I managed to narrow the selection down to two, each of which offers a unique experience. Together, they represent an excellent cross section, if by no means a complete survey, of what New Zealand has to offer the sea kayaker.

MARLBOROUGH SOUNDS

To introduce the first destination, I need to begin with the greatest explorer of the Pacific Ocean, Captain James Cook, who made three exhaustive voyages of discovery in the 1760s and 1770s before his untimely violent end in Hawaii in 1779. On his first journey, in H.M.S. *Endeavor,* he surveyed the entire coast of New Zealand with such precision that his charts were still considered authoritative over a century later. During that circumnavigation he anchored *Endeavor* in a lovely, sheltered cove on the north end of South Island. It became a favorite spot, for he was to stop there in his next ship, *Resolution,* no fewer than four times (staying for a total of over 100 days) in the course of charting much of the southern Pacific Ocean.

Looking down from the trekking trail that ascends the steep hills overlooking Ship Cove, as it is now known, you can easily empathize with Cook. Set on the edge of a convoluted region of channels and islands called Marlborough Sounds, Ship Cove radiates tranquility from its green flanks and blue water. The masts of sailboats that anchor within its eastward-facing crescent barely sway when the prevailing westerlies kick up. From the hillside shade of broad-leaved *kohekohe* and *kahikatea* trees you can look across the cove to Motuara Island bird sanctuary—where Cook stood when he claimed the South Island for his king—and beyond, up Queen Charlotte Sound, where ferries run between North and South Island. A 19th-century visitor described it, ". . . like a carpet at your feet, in endless gradations of light and shade, the New Zealand bush spreads outward in green waves to the edge of the ocean." This is subtropical New Zealand at its most lush.

Four hundred miles south of the Marlborough Sounds, a contrast as great as that between a Victorian high tea and a Maorian war party awaits in Fiordland National Park.

Milford Sound, heart of Fiordland National Park on the west coast of South Island.

FIORDLAND NATIONAL PARK

Fiordland is one of the largest national parks in the world, at over three million acres—but that seemingly impressive two-dimensional measurement offers scant clue to the actual surface area encompassed by this unrelentingly three-dimensional landscape, where cliffs rise straight out of the sea to heights of a half-mile or more, and

NEW ZEALAND'S FLIGHTLESS BIRDS—PAST AND PRESENT

The first Maori to colonize New Zealand found an easy source of meat: an enormous flightless bird we know as the moa. The moa was probably the tallest bird that ever lived, but it had not evolved to deal with a cunning, bipedal predator. The Maori hunted the moa for both food and feathers, and soon drove it to extinction—one of the most well-known case studies of extinction caused by humans.

Today, a relative of the moa, also flightless, survives—but this one is less than two feet tall. There are three species of kiwi in New Zealand, all of them nocturnal and secretive; nevertheless, the kiwi has become the symbol of the entire country. Kiwis sleep

for up to 20 hours every day, spending the rest of the time probing for worms with long beaks, near the tip of which are nostrils tuned to the scent of subterranean prey. The female kiwi is famous among ornithologists for producing a single egg that is fully 25 percent of her own mass—the equivalent of a human mother giving birth to a 30-pound baby.

In Fiordland National Park is another flightless bird, the extremely endangered takahe, which was in fact thought to be extinct for 50 years until its rediscovery in 1948 in the Murchison Mountains. Extensive conservation and captive breeding programs have helped expand its numbers to perhaps 200.

Top: Cathedral Cove, Coromandel Peninsula, North Island.
Above: The climate at the north end of North Island is akin to that of Fiji.

waterfalls tumble from clefts every few hundred yards. The sharp-edged, glacier-scoured valleys and mountain ridges lend a raw, edge-of-the-world feel to Fiordland—fitting given its bluff front on the fractious Tasman Sea, which regularly batters the outer parapets of the park with massive storms. Fortunately the narrow fjords that wind dozens of miles inland are isolated from the worst of the open-sea weather.

Fiordland National Park is well known among trekkers because of the Milford Track, which has been called the finest walk in the world. During the austral summer the Milford Track must be heavily regulated to control foot traffic. But the precipitous nature of Fiordland's terrain creates a sharp population drop between the crowded, groomed walking routes with their tidy huts, and the nearly inaccessible outer fjords of the park. Negotiating the narrow offshoots of Doubtful Sound or Dusky Sound, you feel as though you were present at the creation of the world; the peaks seem fresh-sprung from the sea, with edges as yet undulled by erosion, and the torrents of antediluvian deluges pouring from their flanks. The remote, sub-Arctic feel is hammered home when you stroke past a colony of crested penguins on a rock island. Even the trees clinging to the slopes are ancient: podocarps, with tiny pinelike cones and narrow leaves, date back to the dinosaurs, before flowering plants evolved.

DESCRIBING JUST TWO places to kayak in New Zealand is like suggesting a pair of museums to visit in Washington, D.C.—it hardly does justice to the place. Perhaps New Zealand is ready for a latter-day James Cook; a sea kayaker willing to survey the paddling possibilities of the whole country, from the cockpit of the H.M.S. *Endeavor II.*

SUGGESTED ROUTES

Note that the physical and mental challenge ratings for paddling in New Zealand depend entirely on your route. Degree of difficulty ranges from 1 in sheltered coves to 4 for exposed coastal routes

MARLBOROUGH SOUNDS

With over 800 miles of shoreline, Marlborough Sounds allows sea kayakers a vast choice of uncrowded wilderness routes and primitive campsites. The convoluted nature of the coast, and the frequency of sand beaches, means it's easy to find sheltered paddling and good landing sites.

I suggest seven days for an exploration of Marlborough Sounds, but if you'd like time for more hiking and side paddles, two weeks wouldn't be wasted.

You can also embrace a sybaritic approach in Marlborough and plan a lightly loaded tour to take in some of the beautiful, small coastal lodges nestled into secluded bays along the larger channels, such as Queen Charlotte. From the port town of Picton—which has stores, campgrounds, and hotels—or the isthmus town of Portage it's easy to hire water taxis to ferry you and your boats to put-in sites such as Ship Cove or Cape Jackson if you prefer a one-way paddle (it's better to be ferried out, then you can take your time returning and not worry about a timed rendezvous).

If you have advanced open-water paddling skills, I suggest the loop out of Admiralty Bay around D'Urville Island, to see its resident colonies of New Zealand fur seals and offshore pods of dusky and common dolphins, with the possibility of an orca sighting as well. It's about a 40-mile round-trip from the put-in at French Pass, on the west side of Admiralty Bay. You can also start in Portage and undertake a circumnavigation of nearly the entire Marlborough Sounds region, by way of Cape Jackson, around Forsyth Bay, and back through Pelorus Sound to Portage, roughly 60 miles in all. These loops past exposed headlands assume both skill and detailed local weather reports. But you'll have bitten off your own small piece of Cook's legacy.

FIORDLAND NATIONAL PARK

As you might expect from the physical description, the logistics of paddling Fiordland are intimidating. This is an area where even the self-sufficient are better off going with an organized tour. Only a few companies have taken up the challenge of leading sea kayak trips in Fiordland; most are based in the town of Te Anau, on the edge of the park, and use a powerboat to ferry equipment across the huge Lake Manapouri, followed by a shuttle to reach a put-in on an arm of one of the fjords.

If you're tempted to think that a guide is

One of the quiet coves ringing Queen Charlotte Sound, South Island.

unnecessary, remind yourself that when James Cook probed into these fjords in *Endeavor*, he failed to find a safe anchorage after repeated attempts, only succeeding three years later in *Resolution*. When you explore the end of the world, it doesn't hurt to take advantage of local knowledge.

WHAT TO EXPECT

Whatever you do, don't treat New Zealand like a suburb of Australia. It's a fiercely independent country. That said, New Zealanders ("Kiwis") resemble the Aussies in their friendliness and dashing attitude. You'll find few, if any, cultural barriers here.

The mountain flanks that rise abruptly from the shore in Fiordland can funnel williwaws—powerful gusts of wind that hit the surface of the water almost vertically.

I've listed the prime travel time as November through April, but I especially recommend February and later, when the school holidays are over and there are fewer people out trekking.

You can reach Picton, at the south end of Marlborough Sounds, by ferry from Auckland on North Island.

In addition to numerous deserted beaches, there are scattered private lodges, some with attached campgrounds, in the Marlborough Sounds region, especially in the popular Queen Charlotte Sound area. Camping is not allowed in certain heavily used spots, for example Ship Cove. Ask for advice at the Marlborough Sounds Adventure Company in Picton.

Paddling conditions vary as much in New Zealand as they do along the Pacific Coast of the United States. Water temperatures can exceed 70°F in the north, but will be 20 degrees colder in the southern fjords. A thermal stretch top and bottom is a versatile paddling outfit if you plan to visit several spots.

Although it's easy to find sheltered paddling water amid the fjords and channels of New

MAORI, MUTTONBIRDS, AND MOUNTAINS

A rare example of a strong treaty drafted for the exclusive benefit of a native population is the 1864 agreement regarding the hunting of muttonbirds on and around Stewart Island, the southernmost landmass of New Zealand. Only Maori who are direct descendents of the original owners of Stewart, or their spouses, are allowed to harvest the fat muttonbird (sooty shearwater) chicks in March of each year, shortly before they fledge from burrows dug by the parent birds. The muttonbird is considered a delicacy among Maori, perhaps as much because the

hunt represents a successfully preserved tradition as because of taste.

Another example of intercultural cooperation is permanently attached to the highest mountain in New Zealand. Originally called Aoraki, which means cloud-piercer, the peak was renamed after James Cook by Captain J. L. Stokes in 1852. By means of a treaty and ceremony in 1997, the mountain was formally returned to the Maori for one day. They renamed it, not Aoraki, but Aoraki-Cook, thus paying tribute both to their own traditions and the memory of a great explorer.

Zealand's coast, the steep mountain flanks that rise so abruptly from the shore can often funnel *williwaws*—powerful gusts of wind that can hit the surface of the water almost vertically. If you can hear wind blowing, or see trees on the hillsides waving erratically, watch the water's surface carefully for swirling patterns of air movement, and be prepared to brace quickly. Since williwaws are nearly impossible to predict, it's best to sit out such conditions on shore if possible.

Weather varies too, but in general rainfall is high, so make sure you carry a waterproof tent, big enough to prevent claustrophobia if you're stuck inside for hours at a time. I suggest one with large screen panels to furnish both ventilation and bug protection when air temperatures are warm. Sand flies are a considerable nuisance in some areas, with complaints on record from travelers as far back as Cook. Fortunately, they cannot bite through clothing, so long-sleeved shirts and pants tucked into boots are an effective defense when combined with insect repellent for exposed skin.

GUIDES AND OUTFITTERS

The Marlborough Sounds Adventure Company runs a three-day paddling trip in Marlborough

Sounds. They also rent kayaks. Naturally New Zealand (64-3-573-6078) offers a three-day combination paddle and walk in the Marlborough Sounds area. Fiordland Wilderness Experiences leads trips in Fiordland National Park starting at two days.

MARLBOROUGH SOUNDS ADVENTURE COMPANY

The Waterfront, P.O. Box 195
Picton, New Zealand
64-3-573-6078
www.marlboroughsounds.com

FIORDLAND WILDERNESS EXPERIENCES

66 Quintin Drive
Te Anau, New Zealand
64–318–7540
www.fiordlandseakayak.co.nz

RECOMMENDED READING

■ *TRAMPING IN NEW ZEALAND,* Jim DuFresne (1998. $17.95. Lonely Planet.) Although oriented toward trekking, the information is useful for any independent traveler.
■ *LOST PARADISE, THE EXPLORATION OF THE PACIFIC,* Ian Cameron (1987. Salem House. Out of print.) Brilliant overview of regional history.

Daytrips

San Francisco Bay

atives of San Francisco know that the bay that shares the city's name does not share its peaceful, flowers-in-your-hair personality. The massive tidal flows that fill and empty the bay twice each day create some of the most challenging sea kayaking conditions on the planet, just a few hundred yards from where tourists idly munch their shrimp cocktails and gaze out at Alcatraz Island. And when an outgoing tide slams into incoming ocean swells, the seas near the Golden Gate Bridge can turn downright dangerous.

Nevertheless, it's quite possible to undertake a relaxing paddle of some of San Francisco's sights; the secret is in the timing. First, unless you are a very experienced paddler, you should pick a time of the month near neap tides; that is, when the moon is near its first or last quarter phase. Tides near the full and new moon are higher and faster. Second, buy a tidal chart of the bay, available at any marine supply store in the bay area, and time your paddle to take advantage of the tidal flow, or to avoid as much of it as possible. Stay near shore and away from the mouth of the bay near the Golden Gate. Finally, wear a wet suit; the water is very cold.

A great place to launch for a day trip in San Francisco is right in Aquatic Park, near the Fisherman's Wharf hub of the tourist district. The beach is gentle and sandy, and the water protected. You can paddle out and look at the historic ships moored in the park, then head east toward

downtown to take in the skyline. You'll pass by Pier 39 and its restaurants, and the dozens of Califonia sea lions that have asserted squatters' rights on a couple of the docks. Round the point and paddle under the Bay Bridge, south of which are several ramps where you can land, or return to Aquatic Park. You can also head west of the park and take out at Crissy Field, just short of the Golden Gate.

Total distance is only 6 or 7 miles, but you'll have had a great waterfront view of the best of downtown San Francisco.

The Queensland Coast

*Where tropical forest and barrier reef match
wonders with each other.*

One of the best things about exploring the natural world is the perspective it gives you on the hubris of humans.
We tend to think of ourselves as holding all the
records for grand undertakings and sophisticated technical achievements, but the fact is
that most of our innovations were presaged by
evolution millions of years before we thought
of them. Flight? Well, that's an obvious one.
Electricity? Been done. Chemical warfare?
Yesterday's news. The list goes on and on.

Yet we still fall prey to our assumptions—
especially when it comes to assembling large,
complex objects. For example, if you asked a
cross section of people to name the largest thing
ever constructed by living beings, you'd probably
receive an array of answers ranging from the pyr-
amids to the Great Wall of China to the World
Trade Center to the U.S.S. *Eisenhower*. In fact, not
only are all those choices far from the truth, but

The Whitsunday Islands. Most of the 74 islands in the group remain uninhabited.

if you glued them all together they still wouldn't be close. The largest thing ever built by living beings on earth is the Great Barrier Reef off Australia's northeastern (Queensland) coast. Up to 60 miles across and nearly 1,200 miles in length, it dwarfs by millions of tons anything we puny humans have put together. And while the inquisitive skeptic might discover that marine biologists actually consider the Great Barrier Reef to comprise some 2,900 closely spaced individual reefs, each of *those* is bigger than anything we've ever built.

And what about that term "complex"? Surely a reef can't compare to, say, an aircraft carrier in complexity? Perhaps not. Yet the Great Barrier Reef is built of or forms a substrate for over 400 types of coral; it is home to 1,500 species of fish, 4,000 species of mollusks (oysters, clams, squid, and octopus), even 16 species of sea snake. Like an aircraft carrier, it represents an interdependent entity of astonishing intricacy and efficiency.

The hundreds of islands that pepper the backbone of the reef and the waters nearer the mainland boast their own diversity. Some of these islands are true coral formations; others are continental islands (originally part of the mainland, separated by rising sea levels); one, Fraser Island, is the world's largest sand island. On and around the islands ornithologists have counted over 215 species of birds.

The superlatives of the Great Barrier Reef are well known to anyone who watches television nature programs. But the Queensland coast guarded by the reef is just as fascinating, in part because of the utter disparity to be found there. It's likely that nowhere else on earth is there such a contrast between development and wilderness, a gulf separating one landscape utterly transformed by man from another that man has found almost impossible to change.

On one hand there is the Gold Coast, a 20-mile stretch of shoreline in the far south of Queensland (near Brisbane), which could easily be mistaken for Palm Beach or Honolulu. Hundreds of high-rise resorts crowd shoulder to shoulder, spilling thousands of tanned tourists onto the sunbaked sand. Four million visitors

AT A GLANCE

Trip Length 7–10 days	Price Range (independent trip) $425–$700
Paddling Distance 60 miles	Price Range (outfitted group trip)
Physical Challenge 1 ② 3 4 5	$395–$860
Mental Challenge 1 ② 3 4 5	Staging City Cairns, Australia
Prime Time April–October (cool season in Southern Hemisphere)	

Cape York Peninsula is tropical, bordered with white sand beaches fringed with palms.

pletely inaccessible by vehicle as the tracks turn to bottomless quagmire; even in the dry season only the most robust 4x4s, usually traveling in convoys, can make it through to Cape York itself. The rain forest in the interior is nearly impenetrable to normal travel and is known for its healthy population of venomous snakes (Australia is the only continent in the world where venomous species outnumber nonvenomous ones).

The coast of the peninsula is easily accessible by boat, and there are plenty of beaches on which to land. But there's the little matter of crocodiles, which grow longer than sport utility vehicles here and consider humans just another item on the menu. The numerous mangrove estuaries that dot the coastline north of Cape Melville are ideal habitat for these huge reptiles. The combination of inimical wildlife and inconvenient travel has kept the Cape York Peninsula one of the world's last great wildernesses.

Fortunately, there is a middle ground on the Queensland coast (between crocs and crowds, so to speak), and it happens to be an ideal introduction to the land and seascape of tropical Australia. From Port Douglas, about 40 miles north of Cairns (pronounced *Cans* if you're there), a beautiful, nearly pristine coastal paddling route extends north for 60 miles to Cooktown. Part of the route is bordered by Cape Tribulation National Park, where coastal coconut palms and casuarina trees give way to curtain figs, milky pine, ash, and dozens of other rain forest species, all hung with lianas. Yet much of the forest here is open enough to walk through without trouble. The lucky and observant might spot a cassowary (see box opposite) or koala among the trees or, in the air above the demarcation between sea and forest, a sea eagle or a nankeen kestrel. Offshore are several islands with small fringing reefs that are ideal for impromptu snorkeling capsizes (this is the only place on the planet where two UNESCO World Heritage Areas—the Wet Tropics and the Great Barrier Reef—meet). Past

come here every year to see and be seen lounging on the beach, surfing, or browsing the expensive shops filled with the finest luxury goods. Many of the islands off the Gold Coast sport their own resorts, and the waterways in between are jammed with yachts, powerboats, and personal watercraft (an inoffensive euphemism for those offensive jet-ski things).

Contrast this hedonistic scene with the wilderness of the Cape York Peninsula 800 miles north. This is tropical Australia. Thick rain forest alternates with drier woodland, bordering white sand beaches, with palm-thatched islands delineating the reef just a few miles offshore. During the wet season the entire peninsula becomes com-

Hinchinbrook Island, a national park, can be circumnavigated by kayak in a few days.

A VERY LARGE BIRD

Here's a trick question: What is Australia's largest land animal? Even expert naturalists could be excused for guessing the kangaroo—but the title holder isn't even a mammal, it's a bird. The cassowary, a member of a loosely related group of flightless birds called ratites, commonly weighs over 140 pounds and has been known to exceed 190.

Cassowaries are striking in appearance, and can be downright frightening viewed up close, especially if you know they can defend themselves with powerful kicks that inflict serious wounds. They have a heavy, black body and a vivid blue neck, short, stout legs, and a head straight out of a dinosaur movie—naked, with a large, bony-looking crest. The wings are vestigial but are armed with several wire-like feathers that help the bird force its way through thick undergrowth. Cassowaries eat mostly fruit, including those of poisonous plants, which they can tolerate thanks to a very short digestive system that passes the toxins before they can be absorbed, and a highly efficient liver.

Only about 1,500 cassowaries remain in Australia, and the rain forest of the Cape York Peninsula is their last stronghold. Despite their size and color, they can be very difficult to spot in the forest. Watch closely, and if you see one. . .don't irritate it.

Cape Tribulation the inland rain forest vegetation blends into drier eucalyptus woodland, and the shore is punctuated by the mangrove estuaries that become more common farther north.

Cooktown is the perfect end to this trip since a road leads from Cooktown back to Port Douglas, obviating the need to paddle back south against the prevailing winds. And on the way south you can visit the Daintree rain forest preserve, and take a crocodile-spotting tour from the safety of a *big* boat.

Wherever you explore in Queensland, if your connections take you through Brisbane take time at the end of the trip for a quick tour of the Gold Coast Highway and its resorts and shops and tourists. After just a few hours there, you might come up with the same nickname a friend of mine did for those fre-

netic shoppers looking for the best tan and the best buys.

Croc bait.

SUGGESTED ROUTES
CAPE YORK PENINSULA

From Port Douglas kayakers usually follow the coast to Cape Tribulation, Weary Bay, Cedar Bay, and Walsh Bay. Islands close to the mainland that are suitable for camping and snorkeling include Snappy Island and Rocky Island.

Cooktown—which counts as the first European settlement in Australia, since James Cook established a camp in 1770 and stayed for several weeks—is the terminus for the introductory tour of the Cape York coast. You can paddle back—against the wind—or do what most paddlers do and arrange a shuttle vehicle

Aborigine man playing the didgeridoo.

AND EVEN LARGER REPTILES

To many people's surprise, biologists generally believe that there are only two predators in the world that will habitually and naturally prey on humans: the polar bear and the crocodile. Most other cases of man-eaters involve either mistaken identity on the part of the animal (that is, great white sharks, which are thought to confuse humans with seals), or wounded, sick, or old animals (lions, leopards, and so forth) that prey on humans when they can no longer pursue their normal prey. Only very infrequently do aberrant, but healthy, big cats make a habit of eating people.

The Australian saltwater crocodile will kill humans without hesitation. However, it is important to realize that such attacks are extremely rare. In fact, saltwater crocodiles have been protected in Australia since 1970, after suffering a drastic population falloff from unregulated hunting for hides in the 1950s and '60s. Experienced travelers who frequent crocodile country take precautions to minimize risks—essentially staying away from the mangrove estuaries that are prime croc habitat. The offshore islands along the Great Barrier Reef are less likely to harbor crocs than the mainland coast.

The track of a croc on a sandy beach is unmistakable: a parallel line of prints with a tail drag in between, usually heading straight into or out of the water. The sight of such a trail from a kayak is a really good tip that you should land elsewhere.

The Great Barrier Reef off Cairns. The entire reef is up to 60 miles across and nearly 1,200 miles long.

back from Cooktown.

Prevailing tradewinds along the Queensland coast in the dry season are from the southeast, meaning a quick trip north and a long slog south if you're paddling back to Port Douglas. The winds normally stay around 20 knots or less, but can reach 30 knots for hours on end at times, raising significant whitecaps.

It's also possible to continue paddling north from Cooktown around Cape Melville across Princess Charlotte Bay, to the little settlement of Port Stewart on the Stewart River, which is accessible from Cairns or Port Douglas by a long, very dusty drive. However, the paddle to Port Stewart crosses better (if that's the correct word) crocodile habitat than the coast farther south, so more strategic planning is necessary. The awesomely accomplished ocean paddlers Karen and Dan Trotter went this way on their impressive kayaking journey all the way to the northern tip of Cape York; they took the precaution of staying as far offshore as possible, hopping through the reef islands, and hitting the mainland only to replenish their water supply. (If you're interested in reading more about their trip, see the October 1997 issue of *Sea Kayaker* magazine).

HINCHINBROOK ISLAND

If you'd like to experience kayaking in Queensland, but don't want to be tied to a shuttle vehicle, I suggest Hinchinbrook Island, which is just off the mainland coast about 120 miles south of Cairns. The entire 100,000 acres of Hinchinbrook is a national park, bisected by an enormous granite spine running the length of the island, rising to the 3,500-foot Mount Bowen, the third highest peak in all of Queensland. The ridgeline also bisects the weather on Hinchinbrook: The west side gets more rain, the east less, so there's rain forest on the western slope of the ridge and mostly dry eucalyptus forest on the east, with mangrove channels near the coasts on both sides. You can circumnavigate Hinchinbrook in two or three days, getting a fascinating sort of minitour of the Cape York habitats on the way.

WHAT TO EXPECT

Cairns, the airline terminus for Queensland paddling, is sort of the Gold Coast in miniature, and Port Douglas seems to want to be a Cairns in miniature. However, both towns have plenty of hotels to base out of, and numerous grocery stores for provisioning, as well as rental vehicles if you want to arrange a shuttle. If you have a folding kayak, you can travel north from Cairns by bus, using Coral Coaches (07-4031-7577).

Despite the growth of the resort industry in Port Douglas, less expensive lodgings in the way of hotels, caravan parks, and hostels still exist. In Cooktown, at the end of your paddle, you can treat yourself at the Sovereign Hotel, which has a pool and bar.

You can camp anywhere along the Cape York coast, but there is a national park campground north of Cape Tribulation at Noah Head, and a couple of lodges as well, which are reached by most travelers via the rain forest road that skirts the coast in places. Most impressive is the Coconut Beach Rainforest Retreat, luxurious and priced accordingly ($200-plus per night).

Sea kayaks are available for rent in Brisbane from the Aussie Sea Kayak Company (which also runs tours). Their website is www.ausseakayak.com.

Paddling early in the morning is a good strategy. Water temperatures are warm, but watch for jellyfish. Most of them, such as the generically named but dangerous "stinger," and Portuguese man-o-war, are not common during the winter months, but use caution at all times. It's a good idea to wear long-sleeved shirts and pants while paddling, both as sun protection and to offer a partial barrier to the nematocysts of any jellyfish that might contact you.

Water is usually available from streams along the Cape York coast, but it should be purified or boiled before drinking. Ask locally about water

A school of crescent-tailed bigeyes, Great Barrier Reef.

availability, and also inquire about precautions for crocodiles, which are present in the Daintree River, north of Port Douglas.

GUIDES AND OUTFITTERS

Great Expeditions offers three- and seven-day trips along the Queensland coast and barrier islands, all-inclusive from Cairns.

GREAT EXPEDITIONS

P.O. Box 728, 303 Main St.
Lyons, CO 80540
303-823-6653
www.greatexpeditionstravel.com
$395–$860

RECOMMENDED READING

■ *AUSTRALIA HANDBOOK,* Marael Johnson and Andrew Hempstead (2000. $21.95. Moon Travel Handbooks.) A better-than-average general travel guide to the continent.
■ *AUSTRALIA, THE ROUGH GUIDE,* Margo Daly et al (1999. $21.95. The Rough Guides.) Excellent overall guide to Australia, designed for the independent traveler on a budget.

Opposite: The Great Barrier Reef is home to 400 types of coral, 1,500 species of fish, and 4,000 species of mollusks.

Tuktoyaktuk Peninsula

Adventuring on your own north of the Arctic Circle.

he soul of the Arctic is its vastness.

Here there are no trees, and often no hills or mountains, to lend scale and boundary to the view for those accustomed to more limited landscapes. Your eye is free to sweep on and on, clear to where the horizon fades into an unimaginable distance.

For many it is a daunting perspective. Early explorers' adjectives run to "bleak," "monotonous," and "terrifying." "A world unfinished by the hand of its Creator," wrote one. These men were used to the lush forests and ordered towns of Europe, men for whom a civilized landscape was something to strive for, not escape from.

For the modern explorer it is different. Now that civilized landscapes are the rule, the wilderness that remains exerts an attraction on us fully as potent as the fear it inspired in our forebears. And the Arctic—along with its even more remote corollary, the Antarctic—represents the

"A few miles away, a pingo—a gigantic frost heave like a frozen volcano—shouldered its way 200 feet out of the permafrost."

greatest wilderness left on earth. Consider: if you launch a sea kayak from Tuktoyaktuk, an Inuvialuit settlement on the coast of Canada's Beaufort Sea near the Alaskan border, and paddle east along the route of the Northwest Passage, you'll reach the next coastal settlement, Paulatuk, in about a month—assuming you're lucky with ice conditions and weather, and can average around 15 miles every day. Continue past Paulatuk and it's another month or so to the next village. In fact, along the entire 2,300-mile passage—all the way across the top of North America—there are only four permanent settlements. And the islands of the vast Canadian Arctic archipelago are even more sparsely inhabited.

The land and sea between those isolated outposts inspires disparate emotions: exhilaration and dread; sometimes—even frequently— a heady mixture of the two. Such is the nature of travel in places where you are, if not at the mercy of your surroundings, at least their servant, and where the sense of normalcy that is taken for granted in temperate latitudes ceases to exist. Here, at the height of summer, the sun does not rise and set, but describes a low circle around the horizon. Here your compass might indicate north where due west lies. You do not walk *through* forests, but on top of them: Arctic birch and willow trees, decades old, form a springy, three-inch-tall carpet underfoot. The seawater, despite being cold enough to kill you in minutes, supports a chain of life from diatoms to whales. Here plants, birds, and mammals (and, to our occasional dismay, insects) indulge in a 24-hour-a-day frenzy of feeding and breeding during the brief, but productive, growing season.

One warm August morning on the Tuktoyaktuk Peninsula, my wife and I decided to take a day off from paddling. We walked inland until the sights and sounds and scents of the ocean were lost, and we were surrounded by the limitless tundra. The sky was deep cerulean blue, exactly as deep a blue on the horizon as straight overhead. The sun cast the clean, golden Arctic light that inspired the 16th-century Dutch explorer Willem Barents to quote Solomon in his rapture at seeing day break after a dark, cruel winter shipbound in the ice: "The light is sweet, and it is delightful for the eyes to see the sun."

Sightseeing in the Arctic requires a different

AT A GLANCE

TRIP LENGTH 7–14 days	PRICE RANGE (INDEPENDENT TRIP) $700–$1,200
PADDLING DISTANCE 110–200 miles	PRICE RANGE (OUTFITTED GROUP TRIP)
PHYSICAL CHALLENGE ①②③④ 5	Not available
MENTAL CHALLENGE 1 2 3 ④ 5	STAGING CITY Inuvik, Northwest Territories, Canada
PRIME TIME July–early September	

perspective than we are used to—you learn to look either very far away, miles and miles, or very, very close. Roseann and I lay on our stomachs and peered into the miniature forest under our noses. Willow catkins were forming, and pygmy buttercups showed bright yellow between purple oxytrope blossoms. The empty nest of a plover was slowly being dismantled by the breeze.

Sitting up, through our binoculars we scanned across the gentle hills that led inland. A few miles away, a pingo—a gigantic frost heave like a frozen volcano—shouldered its way 200 feet out of the permafrost. Then, somewhat closer, a movement caught our eyes. An Arctic fox, still shedding great clumps of white fur from his brown summer coat, hunted nose down in the tundra, until a pounce and chomping jaws signalled the demise of a mouse. At last we simply lay on our backs with the sun warming our faces and listened to the wind blow across miles of openness.

Later that day we experienced the other face of the Arctic. We took a break from paddling an unruffled sea and broke out the VHF radio for a weather report, which indicated a powerful storm moving east across the Gulf of Alaska. We looked west, but the sky was clear, so we continued paddling. A half hour later, Roseann said "Look behind us." I did, and saw a thin, ominous black line stretched across the horizon. We pushed up the coast until we found a campsite, and pitched the tent, adding extra guylines and pounding the stakes in deep. An hour later we sat inside sipping hot soup

while a 40-knot wind howled outside. At 3:00 A.M. I got up and stuck my head out into the overcast gloom. Six-foot waves were pounding the shore, hurling massive driftwood tree trunks from the Mackenzie River back and forth with each surge. Above me the low, boiling clouds raced past as in a time-lapse film. The forbidding Arctic landscape of 19th-century painter Frederic Church had come to life.

THE SEA KAYAK was born in the Arctic, and its return, in the form of modern synthetic-hulled and folding craft, has opened up vast potential for exploration. Getting those kayaks to the Arctic, however, can be frighteningly expensive. Usually flying is the only practical means of moving equipment and people between points, and flying, along with everything else, costs more at the edge of a frontier.

But there is another way to reach the Arctic: You can simply drive there. Just east of Dawson, in the Yukon Territory of Canada, the Dempster Highway leaves the Alaskan Highway and heads north about 500 miles to Inuvik (Innoovik). This busy supply hub of about 3,000 people on the bank of the Mackenzie River in the Northwest Territories is 200 miles north of the Arctic Circle. It is a rough 500-mile drive of razor-edged gravel and huge speeding semitrailer trucks, but at the end you can drop your kayak in the river and paddle to the Arctic Ocean—and Tuktoyaktuk, the gateway to the Northwest Passage.

Opposite: The author's wife surveys the tundra. The Arctic requires a new perspective; you learn to look either miles and miles away or very close. Above: Kayaks ready to be loaded on the waiting Cessna.

Inuvik is on an eastern side channel of the Mackenzie. You'll stay in this channel all the way to Kugmallit Bay, then simply follow the coast to Tuktoyaktuk. It's about 110 river and sea miles from Inuvik to Tuktoyaktuk.

The Mackenzie north of Inuvik is a placid river of numerous channels, most less than a hundred yards across, widening to a delta mouth. You'll be paddling in the easternmost channel most of the way. It's about 90 miles from Inuvik to where the river empties into Kugmallit Bay on the Beaufort Sea, so you'll get a small (1 to 2 mph) boost from the current for the first several days.

You might be surprised to see sizable stands of spruce here, far north of the normal treeline. Camping spots are sparse due to the dense willow thickets crowding the banks of the river. However, the islands in the channels are sometimes lower and easier to land on than the main banks of the river, so campsites are easier to find there. But once you emerge into Kugmallit Bay, the last vestiges of tall vegetation disappear, and you find yourself amid true Arctic tundra. The horizon recedes and the sweet tang of the Beaufort Sea replaces the earthy smell of the river. If you've pushed hard to get down the river you'll want to take a day off to sample this new

Overlooking the Mackenzie Delta, where the 1,120-mile-long Mackenzie River flows into Kugmallit Bay.

Even with such comparatively easy access, an independent sea kayaking tour in the Arctic is not to be taken lightly. You should be an experienced paddler before considering it, well practiced in recovery and rescue techniques, and have top-notch equipment and clothing. But if you do take on a trip to the Arctic, you will return home with visions of distant horizons in your head, the brisk tang of polar air on your palate, and a sense of having skirted what is even today the edge of the world.

BELUGAS

The most common whale found in the vicinity of Tuktoyaktuk is the beluga, a small (15 to 16 feet) toothed whale, a striking, creamy white in adult coloration (the young are gray). Belugas frequently hunt close to shore, following the tide in and out in their search for small fish. Their habit of spy hopping—rising vertically out of the water to see what's around them—makes them easy to spot. Belugas are perhaps the most highly vocal of all whales, and their

near-constant chatter of squeaks and chirps earned them the nickname "sea canary."

Belugas are still hunted by the Inuit, for whom they are an important food source. Muktuk, small raw chunks of the inner skin and outer layer of fat, or blubber, is a delicacy in the far north. The taste is surprisingly mild, only a bit fishy, with a rather pleasing chewy texture.

environment. There are numerous landing sites, either coarse sand or smooth cobble, always with a rim of driftwood from the river.

Tuk makes a worthy final destination, and you can hire a bush plane or boat to return you and your boats to Inuvik. However, there are further possibilities for exploration northeast along the Tuktoyaktuk Peninsula after resupplying in one of the small stores in town. If you continue beyond Tuk or arrange for a flight to a different base camp, the possibilities are endless.

A short charter flight can also drop you across the peninsula in Liverpool Bay, a convoluted wilderness that presents many paddling possibilities, including paddling back all the way around the Tuktoyatuk Peninsula to Tuk.

WHAT TO EXPECT

Tuktoyaktuk (Tucktoy*ahk*took, or simply Tuk to the locals) won't beguile you with postcard images of northern life. Instead it provides a fascinating, untinted glimpse into the lives of the modern Inuit people, who remain poised between a hunter/gatherer existence and the modern world

BIRDS OF THE MACKENZIE RIVER

The vast majority of Arctic birds are only part-time residents, migrating north in spring to exploit the 24-hour daylight and highly productive habitat. One species you'll see hundreds of on the river is the bank swallow, which arrives from wintering grounds in South America in late May and builds huge communal nesting colonies in vertical riverbanks. Males and females cooperate to dig horizontal burrows as deep as four or five feet, excavating with their bills and kicking the dirt out with their feet. The burrows are often no more than a foot apart, making one wonder how they keep from running into each other. When the burrow is complete, the female lays four or five eggs in a nest of grass and weeds. When you paddle past one of these colonies you'll be surrounded by hundreds of chittering swallows.

Another bird you're likely to see here is generally considered the champion of all migratory animals in the world. Each year Arctic terns fly from the Antarctic continent to the high Arctic to breed, then make the return journey in late summer, a round-trip of around 22,000 miles. Arctic terns live under more daylight than any other animal on earth. While paddling, you'll spot them hovering over the water, looking for small fish to scoop up.

Arctic terns nest in simple, shallow scrapes along flat banks of the Mackenzie, which means you'll sometimes land near one while looking for a campsite or lunch spot. You'll soon know if a nest is close by, because the birds will make repeated, full-throttle dives at your head to drive you off. You should leave immediately to avoid disturbing them further. The nests and eggs are literally invisible from a couple of feet away, so well do they blend in to the substrate.

A curiously shallow rainbow on the Beaufort Sea. Along the entire 2,300-mile coast of the sea—all the way across the top of North America—there are only four permanent settlements.

of boom-and-bust resource-extraction employment. During the oil craze of the 1970s, the town served as a major port and storage center for Beaufort Sea offshore rigs. Employment was high, and per capita income skyrocketed. With the decline in prices during the '80s the activity stopped, and jobs disappeared—but not the hardware, which still forms the skyline of the town, along with the abandoned DEW (Distant Early Warning) line radar dome.

Today the residents of Tuktoyaktuk have returned to at least a partial subsistence economy. They still hunt beluga whales, and the meat is stored in an enormous community freezer, which is simply a series of tunnels bored through the permafrost under the town. Every few years Tuk hosts the Arctic Games, a celebration of life in the Arctic mixed with contests of physical skills. Walking through the town provides a kaleidoscope of images: gaily painted houses on permafrost stilts, muddy streets, and sled dogs staked out next to snowmobiles and Ford trucks (the only way to drive to Tuk is in winter, when the Mackenzie River and the Beaufort Sea freeze over thick enough that even semitrailer trucks make the journey).

Inuvik has several grocery stores where you can buy just about anything you'd need in the way of provisions—for a price typically twice to three times what you'd pay a thousand miles south. Plan carefully. There's also a Great Northern Company store here (formerly Hudson's Bay) with a good selection of hard goods, but no kayaking equipment. There is also a superb bookstore, Boreal Books, with many natural history titles.

For all its glory, the Arctic demands a price

of visitors. As does no other destination in this book, the Arctic requires the utmost skill and self-reliance from the independent paddler. Even in midsummer, water temperatures are cold enough to cause incapacitation in minutes for an unprotected paddler forced to wet exit. A dry suit is the only adequate protection, along with superior boat handling and self-rescue skills. Weather can change suddenly from sunny and calm to overcast, cold, and windy. There is some boat traffic on the Mackenzie, and the crews are *not* used to watching for sea kayaks—it is your responsibility to stay out of the way.

With good weather, the paddle from Inuvik to Tuktoyaktuk is easy on the physical challenge scale. However, further exploration of the Tuktoyaktuk Peninsula or the Liverpool Bay area could quickly escalate the challenge rating to a 5. While there is regular boat traffic on the Mackenzie between Inuvik and Tuktoyaktuk, once you get off the main routes you will be completely isolated, in an environment that leaves little room for error.

Your best line of weather defense on shore is a good-quality tent, either a four-season model or a stout three-season design. (*Please,* no $39.95 dome tents!) A vestibule is a good idea, as it provides an additional mosquito-free area where you can prepare food. Mosquitoes can be a plague at some camps, at others we found virtually none. A breezy campsite helps, as does a head net.

It's remotely possible that you'll cross paths with either polar or grizzly bears (although *most* polar bears stay on the pack ice to the north, they occasionally venture onto the mainland in summer). Cook and store food away from your tent, and carry a large can of at least 10 percent capsicum spray, which should be used only if you are closely menaced by a bear. For capsicum spray to be legally imported into Canada, the canister must state that it is for use on animals. Incidentally, capsicum spray cannot be used as an advance repellent by spraying it on your tent or around camp. The diluted scent will actually *attract* bears, who will assume you are preparing a Mexican dinner for them (or *are* a Mexican dinner for them).

If you drive to Inuvik, keep in mind that gasoline is two to three times as expensive on the Dempster Highway as elsewhere, as is the cost of all other supplies and services.

GUIDES AND OUTFITTERS

There are no commercial sea kayak tours on this route. Organized tours to other parts of the Candadian Arctic are offered by Ecosummer Expeditions (800-465-8884) and start at about $2,000, not including airfare to a hub.

There are several air charter companies in Inuvik. You can sometimes negotiate a better deal if you book the aircraft for what would otherwise be an empty return flight. Try Arctic Wings, which flies to Tuk and other destinations using single-engine Cessnas.

ARCTIC WINGS
P.O. Box 1916
Inuvik, Northwest Territories
Canada X0E 0T0
867-777-2220

RECOMMENDED READING

■ *A NATURALIST'S GUIDE TO THE ARCTIC,* E.C. Pielou (1994. $20.00. University of Chicago Press.) An outstanding introduction to the plants and animals of the north.
■ *ARCTIC DREAMS,* Barry Lopez (1986. $12.95. Bantam.)

Disko Bay

*A birthplace of glaciers, where sea kayaks
still work for a living.*

There's something that sets Greenland apart from any other destination in this book.

It's not the scenery. Certainly, Greenland's coast is striking in its beauty—it's a spare Arctic land of rugged inlets and fjords, turfed with shocking green tundra and punctuated by massive glaciers with towering mountain backdrops—but after all, if you've flipped through the other chapters it should be obvious that beautiful scenery is a dominant theme here. And it's not the remoteness. At least a couple of other areas—Tierra del Fuego, the Tuktoyaktuk Peninsula—offer similar isolation for paddlers who want to challenge a true wilderness.

So what makes Greenland different? Because, while exploring these waters, it's just possible that you'll encounter a native Inuit hunter paddling a handmade, skin-on-frame sea kayak—not for fun, but for work, as his ancestors

Near Etah, northwest Greenland (78 degrees north latitude), where Perry prepared for his polar attempts.

GREENLAND

have done for thousands of years. In fact, our word for kayak comes from the Greenland *Qajaq.*

Greenland was one of the last regions to be colonized by the Thule Culture, ancestors of the modern Inuit people. The Thule were accomplished seafarers who made use of large, open, skin boats up to 30 feet in length, called umiaks, as well as smaller, closed-deck kayaks. The umiak, either rowed or fitted with a square sail, was used for moving household goods and was usually crewed by women, while the men used the lighter, faster kayak for scouting and hunting. The Thule migrated rapidly eastward across the top of Canada during the 10th century A.D., either displacing or absorbing the earlier Dorset peoples, who also used kayaks. The Thule reached northern Greenland at about the same time the Norse seafarers landed their longships in southern Greenland and founded their own settlements.

The Norse settlers, despite their fierce reputation, depended on agriculture for most of their food. They were forced out of Greenland by the Little Ice Age, which began lowering temperatures in the 12th century. The Thule hunters, of course, scoffed at such minor annoyances as ice ages and did just fine. Today, their direct descendents still use kayaks frequently to hunt seals and whales in the cold waters off Greenland's Arctic Coast. In fact, by self-imposed rule the Inuit here hunt narwhals—20-foot-long whales with unicorn-like tusks—only from kayaks, using hand-thrown harpoons. Although the idea of such a hunt seems barbaric to many urbanites, over one fifth of Greenland's population still relies completely on hunting to survive, and low-impact tools such as kayaks and harpoons help ensure the long-term health of the whale population. And as anyone who has accompanied indigenous hunters anywhere can testify, those hunters honor their prey far more than we do the cows whose tidily dissected carcasses we pick through at the supermarket.

THE WORLD'S LARGEST ISLAND (840,000 square miles), with fewer than 60,000 inhabitants, Greenland boasts one of the lowest population densities on earth if you take into account the entire landmass. However, since 90 percent of the

Overleaf: Towering Greenland iceberg at dawn. It was almost certainly a Greenland iceberg that sank the Titanic.

AT A GLANCE

TRIP LENGTH 1–2 weeks	PRICE RANGE (INDEPENDENT TRIP)
PADDLING DISTANCE 70–90 miles	$1,200–$3,200
PHYSICAL CHALLENGE 1 ②③④ 5	PRICE RANGE (OUTFITTED GROUP TRIP)
MENTAL CHALLENGE 1 2 3 ④⑤	$1,000–$3,595
PRIME TIME Late May–September	STAGING CITY Kangerlussuaq, Greenland

Above: Skjoldungun Fjord, Greenland's east coast. One of the most remote wildernesses on earth, its isolated villages are separated by hundreds of miles.

island is covered by a massive permanent ice cap, settlement is clustered along the coast. The vast majority of that settlement is on the west coast, where the northward-flowing West Greenland Current helps keep the offshore waters free of pack ice for several months each summer (although it also carries icebergs along the coast—more attraction than menace for kayakers).

The clustered pattern of settlement in Greenland offers two distinct personalities for the coastal explorer.

If you crave utter solitude, and are up to testing yourself against one of the most remote wildernesses on earth, you can charter an airplane from Nuuk to drop you and your boat at one of the isolated villages on the east coast, most of which are separated by hundreds of miles. This is territory suitable only for expert kayakers possessing the equipment, skills, and experience needed for paddling on the edges of persistent pack ice in mercurial weather conditions. VHF radio communication is impossible along most stretches of the east coast, so you will be utterly on your own unless you carry a satellite telephone or, for last-ditch emergencies, an EPIRB (Emergency Position-Indicating Radio Beacon).

Opposite: Traditional Inuit kayaker on Disko Bay.

I mention the east coast as an example of a possibility for an extremely remote trip for experienced, committed, well-financed paddlers. There are no specific routes and no permanent resupply stops. There are definitely no outfitters.

For paddlers who want to experience Greenland, but can't afford the massive investment in time, money, and commitment required by the east coast routes, the west coast is the place to start, and it is the focus of this chapter.

Don't take the warnings about the east coast as a sign that the west coast of Greenland is some sort of bunny slope. It's still a wilderness, subject to rapid meteorological shifts, with ocean water that hovers near the freezing point even in summer. Nevertheless, the presence of scattered towns and villages allows you to plan a route that includes regular resupply stops, and which lies within VHF range of coastal receivers most of the time so you can receive weather reports.

There are hundreds of possible kayaking routes; in fact, you can paddle straight out of the capital of Greenland, Nuuk, into the labyrinth of fjords behind the port. However, about 350 miles north of the capital is an area that combines some of the best of what Greenland has to offer.

Look at a map of Greenland, about one-third of the way up the west coast, and you'll find the enormous Disko Bay, fully 120 miles from top to bottom and dominated by Disko Island—itself over 70 miles long. The coast of Disko Bay is characterized by numerous, extensive fjords and archipelagoes; the total coastline in this region alone would certainly measure in the thousands of miles.

At nearly 70 degrees north latitude, well above the Arctic Circle, Disko basks under several weeks of midnight sun each summer—although the sky is often overcast, lending an ethereal

GREENLAND'S ICE CAP

The ice sheet that covers 90 percent of Greenland's surface—approximately 700,000 square miles in extent, roughly 14 times the size of England—is up to 11,000 feet thick in places. So massive is this burden that the center of the island has sagged 1,200 feet below sea level. If the ice cap were to melt, the ocean level would rise over 20 feet, innundating every port in the world.

At the perimeter of the island, the ice cap flows downhill in massive glaciers, some of which move as fast as 100 feet per day. When the glaciers reach open water, huge chunks break off into the sea and slowly drift off in the current. Off the west coast of Greenland these icebergs normally drift north for a time with the West Greenland Current, then circle south with the Canadian Current into the Labrador Sea. It was almost certainly an iceberg from Greenland that sank the *Titanic*.

For sea kayakers, a free-floating iceberg normally poses very little threat, although under certain conditions it can capsize without warning as its center of gravity shifts with melting. Remember as you paddle past that about 90 percent of an iceberg's mass is underwater.

Greenland's ice cap has proven extremely valuable to scientists. Through a project known as GRIP (Greenland Icecore Project), they have sampled cores of the ice over 9,000 feet deep. Residue in these cores provides astonishingly detailed clues to climate fluctuations and other events over hundreds of thousands of years. For example, the scientists were able to pinpoint the rapid development of copper smelting in the Mediterranean area 2,500 years ago from minute particles deposited on the ice.

Incidentally, according to data from NASA the ice cap seems to have begun to shrink over the last 20 years, lending further weight to the theory of global warming.

Inuit hunter's kayak used for hunting narwhals. The bundle on rear deck is a sealskin bladder used as a float to prevent whales from diving deeper after they have been harpooned.

blue tint to the hundreds of icebergs floating in the bay. The majority of those bergs originate in one fjord near the town of Ilulissat, on the east side of the bay. In fact, a single glacier there, the Sermeq Kujalleq, calves more icebergs than any glacier in the world, some of them weighing over five million tons. Paddling near the Sermeq Kujalleq would be suicidal—besides, there's more ice than water in that fjord.

A good base camp for exploring the Disko region is Aasiaat, a fishing community and cargo terminus on a small island at the south end of the bay, accessible from Nuuk either by aircraft or passenger ship. Looking north from Aasiaat over the drifting icebergs you can see the mountains of Disko Island, more than 40 miles away. Out of sight over the forbidding horizon of Davis Strait to the west is Baffin Island. And south is a dense cluster of islands and scattered fishing villages that's perfect for exploring by kayak.

Archaeological evidence suggests human habitation in the Aasiaat archipelago spans over 6,000 years. It's easy to see why: In addition to the rich abundance of marine and bird life, much of the water is sheltered from the open sea, and safe landing spots with cobble beaches and good natural campsites are abundant. On the islands, Arctic foxes stalk nesting grouse, and trout swim in the streams that tumble down through the dark rocks. It's a perfect place to step into the mind of a kayak hunter of ages past.

As for the present, the people of Greenland are undergoing a fascinating transition into the modern world of e-mail and cell phones, while clinging—by necessity as well as preference—to thousands of years of tradition. Nowhere is this more evident than in a commercial you might see if you turn on the television in your hotel. A man in a traditional sea kayak paddles out to a small iceberg and attacks it with carving tools. When he finishes, he paddles away and the camera shows us his creation: a large, icy Coca-Cola bottle, bobbing in the Arctic water.

SUGGESTED ROUTES

From Aasiaat there are literally hundreds of possible routes in the maze of channels to the south. Paddle east from Aasiaat around the end of its island, then cross the narrow channel to the big island of Saqqarluup Nunaa. Just west is a convoluted inlet sheltered from almost all rough water, with gentle beaches suitable for landing and camping.

If the weather is clear, you can continue around the west point of Saqqarluup Nunaa, taking in the imposing view of Davis Strait to the west, and then head back east along the south coast of the island. From there you can either aim for a circumnavigation of Saqqarluup Nunaa (there's a short portage involved if the tide is low), or cross over to any of the dozens of smaller islands to the south—a labyrinth of passages where it's easy to become disoriented but difficult to get lost if you pay attention. (The most difficult navigational trick in the Arctic is learning *not* to use the sun for position, since it circles the sky rather than bisects it on a predictable east to west track.) It's about a two-mile jump from Saqqarluup Nunaa to an archipelago of about a dozen small islands headed by a tiny one called Portukullak. From the archipelago you can cross to one of three larger islands: Umiluik, Kannala, or Naajat. Kannala is separated from the mainland only by a narrow strait.

You'll see a few fishing villages and camps in the Aasiaat region, including many that are abandoned and fun to explore. Greenlanders are friendly and extremely hospitable, but often quiet—long periods of silence during conversation are considered normal, and when it's time to leave you'll sometimes find yourself politely ignored. Don't be insulted, and don't try to fill in every gap with pointless talk.

WHAT TO EXPECT

Regularly scheduled airline flights from Canada land at the international airport in Kangerlussuaq, the major transportation hub on the west coast, about halfway up. From there you can take a regularly scheduled de Havilland turboprop directly

UNICORNS OF THE SEA

When pieces of the graceful, spiral, ivory tusks of narwhal whales began showing up in Europe in the Middle Ages, they were taken as obvious proof of the existence of unicorns, and soon the few existing examples were selling for 20 times their weight in gold. Not until the 17th century was a new species of whale recognized as the real source.

The narwhal's tusk, which is a highly modified tooth usually found only in males, can grow up to eight or nine feet long. Its purpose is still unclear, although since it is a male characteristic, most theories suggest its use as a weapon for establishing dominance and defending harems. Normally the tusk grows from the left side of the narwhal's head; occasionally a second, smaller, tusk will grow from the right side.

Narwhals, which are closely related to belugas, grow up to about 18 feet long and weigh over 3,000 pounds. They are usually found in groups, and will dive together to depths of over 1,000 feet to hunt cod and redfish. In turn, narwhals are preyed on by orcas and Greenland sharks, as well as Inuit hunters.

to Aasiaat. You can also book passage on one of the Arctic Umiaq Line's passenger/cargo ships that serve the west coast communities. These ships are sort of the interstate bus system of Greenland.

Information about accommodations and other practicalities in Greenland is not as hard to come by as you might think. The government hosts an excellent website at www.greenland-guide.gl.

There are several hotels and cafes in Aasiaat. You can also rent fiberglass kayaks and gear for an independent trip; find out more through the Greenland website, which has a link to Aasiaat.

This is the Arctic, and all paddling rules for extremely cold water apply. A dry suit with a fleece underlayer is mandatory for immersion protection. You should be well practiced (and *fast*) in self- and assisted-rescue techniques. If you're camping on your own, I recommend a sturdy four-season tent to handle strong winds.

Weather conditions in Greenland can change with dramatic suddenness. Plan crossings and transits of rocky lee shores with care. Carry a VHF radio to obtain weather information when in range of transmitters.

There are mosquitoes in Greenland, and they can be annoying in certain areas. A head net is the best defense if you find yourself besieged. Breezy campsites are better than calm ones.

GUIDES AND OUTFITTERS

Aasiaat Tourist Services offers an all-inclusive tour of the Aasiaat archipelago. Ibex Expeditions runs a trip to northwest Greenland from Resolute, in the Northwest Territories. Both are mostly camping, with some nights in small hotels or lodges

AASIAAT TOURIST SERVICES
299-89-25-40
$1,000 for 8 days
IBEX EXPEDITIONS
800-842-8139
$3,595 for 17 days

Top: Near Smith Sound by Ellesmere Island. Pack ice can force kayakers to drag their boats for many miles. Above: An Inuit on Disko Bay.

RECOMMENDED READING

- *ARCTIC DREAMS,* Barry Lopez (1986. $12.95. Bantam.) His best work; a personal exploration of the people, landscape, and history of the Arctic.
- *ICE!,* Tristan Jones (1995 reprint. $13.95. Sheridan House Books.) An astonishing account of a penniless Welsh sailor's attempt to sail closer to the North Pole than anyone in history.

Tierra del Fuego

Test your paddling skills among the glaciers at the end of the earth.

The winds and seas that hammer the west coast of the southern tip of South America have built in strength for thousands of miles, unfettered by a single other landmass for the entire circumference of the earth. Waves that would be legendary in the North Atlantic Ocean—50 and 60 feet from trough to crest—are commonplace in the Drake Passage, the 500-mile channel that separates South America from Antarctica. Sailors refer to this latitude in the Southern Hemisphere as the "furious fifties" and still consider the passage around Cape Horn, the storm-battered cliffs at the very end of the continent, to be the ultimate test of seamanship, and of the boat itself. No one has a count of the number of ships lost off this shore in the last 500 years, but the victims range from early square-riggers to the most modern sail and power craft.

Fortunately, as Ferdinand Magellan discovered in 1520, the tip of South America is not a

Paddling toward the head of Bahia Brookes. Here the sound of ice cracking and booming is ever-present.

CHILE

ARGENTINA

ATLANTIC

Strait of Magellan

Punta Arenas • • Porvenir

PACIFIC

TIERRA DEL FUEGO
Parque Nacional Tierra del Fuego
Ushuaia• *Darwin Range*

single landmass, but an archipelago laced with dozens of channels, sheltered—at least to some extent—from the apocalyptic furies of the open sea. On his quest to complete the first circumnavigation of the earth, Magellan traversed the straits now named after him from the Atlantic Ocean to the Pacific. As his ship sailed beneath the towering snowcapped mountains flanking the channel, and past fjords headed by massive glaciers, he and his men noted in amazement the smoke from hundreds of fires kept burning along the shore by the native Yahgan and Alacalufe Indians to combat the cold. Thus, in spite of ice, snow, and frigid seas, Magellan dubbed the country *Tierra del Humo*—Land of Smoke. However, King Charles V of Spain, Magellan's sponsor, apparently thought that lacked a bit of impact, because he renamed the place *Tierra del Fuego*—Land of Fire. It does have more punch, doesn't it?

Three hundred years after Magellan's voyage, when Charles Darwin explored Tierra del Fuego in the course of his journey on the *Beagle*, he wrote down his first impressions: "A single glance was sufficient to show me how widely different it was from anything I had ever beheld." It's a phrase that will echo in the thoughts of sea kayakers who brave this most remote corner of the Western Hemisphere.

It begins with the light. Whether the sky is clear and sunny or, as is often the case, overcast with that dense ceiling of gray that seems as though it must encompass the world, the light in the unpolluted southern sky shines with a soft, even radiance, like perfect stage lighting for the dramatic set backdrops of mountains, forests, glaciers, and waterfalls. The air is so transparent that, as in the Arctic, faraway objects do not fade from view—they simply become smaller and smaller until the human eye can no longer resolve them.

The landscape illuminated by this perfect light is deserving of the honor. The Cordillera Darwin, the mountains that form the spine of the main island of Tierra del Fuego, rise almost directly from the sea to heights of over 8,000 feet. The lower slopes are covered in dense beech forest colored such a deep green it is almost black; the upper slopes and peaks hide under a permanent cloak of snow. Waterfalls, many of them hundreds of feet high, glow incandescently white against the glistening onyx of the granite clefts through which they surge.

AT A GLANCE

TRIP LENGTH 2–12 days	PRICE RANGE (INDEPENDENT TRIP) $425–$2,100
PADDLING DISTANCE 20–100 miles	PRICE RANGE (OUTFITTED GROUP TRIP)
PHYSICAL CHALLENGE 1 2 3 4 (5)	$220–$1,290
MENTAL CHALLENGE 1 2 3 4 (5)	STAGING CITY Punta Arenas, Chile
PRIME TIME Mid-November–March	

Not all of Tierra del Fuego is glacier-clad, nor are all of the waters surrounding it littered with icebergs.

The players on this dramatic stage are animals in a variety that must have bewildered a pre-*Origin of Species* Charles Darwin. In how many places on earth can you watch Magellanic penguins frolicking offshore, then turn where you stand and spot parakeets flitting through the forest? Or watch a southern right whale spouting in a fjord, then look up to see guanacos—relatives of camels—bouncing with apparent suicidal intent down a sheer cliff? Look higher and you might spy an Andean condor soaring on a ten-foot wingspan. There are also foxes and even cougars in the forests, and elephant seals on some beaches.

But it is perhaps the acoustical accompani-ment to the whole scene that is Tierra del Fuego's most awe-inspiring feature. In the hundreds of fjords headed by massive glaciers flowing down from the peaks, the sound of ice is an ever-present theme: Far-off cracks and booms, like distant artillery, signal the movement and adjustments of the ice, while nearby roars and sudden, tearing percussives mark the violent birth of an iceberg plunging into the black water. A rising hiss approaches steadily, then surges past, as a wave displaced by a big berg sweeps the shoreline clear of untethered kayaks and carelessly dropped gear.

The logistics and, yes, hazards of mounting an independent kayaking expedition to Tierra del

Fuego are significant, but the reward is a memory of experiences in a land just this side of creation. If you go on your own you should be an expert paddler with superb self-rescue skills; otherwise it is much safer to sign up with one of the few companies running guided trips in southern Chile.

My best advice on visiting Tierra del Fuego is to leave it until you're well along in your paddling career. Once you've been, it's likely to become the standard by which you judge all future trips.

SUGGESTED ROUTES

From Punta Arenas two major options beckon the independent sea kayaker. You can fly across the strait and into Argentine Tierra del Fuego, to the town of Ushuaia, directly on the Beagle Channel (named for Darwin's ship) and less than 10 miles east of Parque Nacional Tierra del Fuego. Ushuaia is a growing town with several hotels and hostels, and you can paddle directly out of the harbor to explore the park. Although much of the coast is wilderness, camping in the park is allowed only in a half-dozen designated campgrounds. The tourist office in Ushuaia has complete information.

An even more strenuous and remote route is accessible with folding kayaks and a rental car. From Porvenir a very rough road winds south along the Tierra del Fuego coast, skirting the huge Bahia Inútil, through Camerón, to the little settlement of Puerto Arturo. From here you can paddle south south along the coast about 10 miles into a 60-mile-long inlet called Seno Almirantazgo, which lances southeast into the heart of Tierra del Fuego. Along the southern shore of the inlet are three elongated bays (bahias) between 8 and 25 miles in length: Brookes, Ainsworth, and Parry. These bays, directly underneath Mount Darwin and Mount Mayo, boast some of the largest glaciers in the region. They're mostly deserted, and have many stretches of safe landing spots with excellent camping sites.

The beaches in Brookes, Ainsworth, and Parry bays are gently sloping for the most part, but there's little sand—it's all glacial rubble, from smooth pebbles to rough boulders, so take

Overleaf: Bahia Ainsworth, beneath Mount Darwin, boasts some of the largest glaciers in the region.

PENGUINS

Penguins, the flightless, tuxedoed birds of so many cartoons, are found only in the Southern Hemisphere, the near exception being the Galapagos penguin. Of eighteen species, two, the Humboldt penguin and the Magellanic penguin, are found in South America. Magellanic penguins are common in Tierra del Fuego, and can be spotted cavorting in the roughest seas in large groups. They spend much of their lives in the water, but come ashore in spring to nest, either under bushes or in burrows, which they defend with vigor. However, a patient observer can sit nearby and often see them emerge to inspect the intruder. Magellanic penguins, like all their relatives, are monogamous and mate for life, and the male takes part in rearing the young.

Magellanics are medium-sized penguins, about 20 inches tall (far smaller than the giant emperor penguins of Antarctica, which stand four feet high and weigh up to 70 pounds). Their diet consists largely of the same krill eaten by baleen whales. They pursue their tiny prey by literally flying through the water, using their wings as flippers and reaching speeds of up to 10 miles per hour.

You might spot penguins nearly anywhere in Tierra del Fuego. About 25 miles north of Punta Arenas is Isla Magdalena, a penguin preserve where a colony of about 50,000 birds live.

care when landing. Pay close attention to tides as well, as the range can exceed 15 feet. You'll also run into areas within the bays that are almost choked solid with small chunks of ice through which you have to force your way.

If the weather is exceptionally clear, you can cross Seno Almirantazgo (about 10 miles of exposed paddling) to Bahia Brookes at the head of the sound, or go farther up where it is narrower. If a long crossing becomes out of the question, you have to paddle all the way up the sound about 50 miles to the abandoned logging town of Rio Azopardo at its end, then back along the southern coast—a long detour, but safer. Keep in mind the prevailing southwesterly winds, which make the north coast of Seno Almirantazgo a lee shore.

WHAT TO EXPECT

The archipelago of Tierra del Fuego, some 30,000 square miles in extent (roughly the size of Ireland), is divided between the countries of Chile and Argentina. Punta Arenas, a Chilean town on an isthmus of the mainland across the Strait of Magellan from the main island of Tierra del Fuego, is the logical base for most exploration. Punta Arenas is a busy town (population about 110,000) of red-roofed buildings, some-

what bleak in the cold and wind, but possessing a certain European charm that offsets its industrial nature. Car rental agencies in Punta Arenas rent sturdy Fiats, suitable for banging around the local roads, and a car ferry crosses the 25-mile-wide strait to the small tin-clad town of Porvenir on Tierra del Fuego.

Some bad news: If you happen across inlets or coves where fishermen or scallop divers have set up temporary camps, you might be appalled at the litter and general filth. It's sometimes difficult to rationalize the cultural differences involved, but if the fishermen or divers are there, don't act offended or superior. It's their land, and they lack the efficient waste disposal industry we take for granted.

Paddling in Tierra del Fuego, whether or not you are part of an organized expedition or guided tour, requires the absolute best in paddling gear, protective clothing, rescue equipment, and skill. A dry suit is mandatory; I recommend neoprene booties with overboots, and neoprene gloves with pogies. The water temperature in open channels averages around 40°F, and in ice-choked fjords it can be barely above freezing. Be extremely conservative when planning crossings, as winds can increase from dead calm to 40 or 50 knots in minutes.

A FERTILE LAND

Although Tierra del Fuego seems harsh to us, it is actually a highly productive ecosystem. The Magellanic forest receives between 120 and 135 inches of rain per year, nourishing the dense groves of beech as well as the ferns underneath, such as the striking *Blechnum magellanicum,* with leaves that are dark green on the outside and pink near the trunk. In spite of harsh winters, spring wildflowers attract several species of hummingbird. River otters cavort in the hundreds of

streams that tumble down the slopes, and nutrias—large rodents that feed on fish and crustaceans—can sometimes be seen on the shore. Offshore the mammal life is just as diverse, from fur seals and Commerson's dolphins up to the largest creature ever to live on earth: the blue whale. And in between the whales' territory and the nutrias', you might spot a *Pato Quetro* (paddlewheel duck), a flightless duck that propels itself by using its wings as paddles.

Elephant seals on a small island off the coast of Tierra del Fuego. Prime bulls can weigh up to 10,000 pounds.

Beware of large masses of kelp found in some areas. In rough seas, kelp can snare your paddle and catch the bow of the kayak as it surfs down waves. Also beware of freefloating icebergs, which can shift position or even capsize due to melting beneath the waterline.

Observing glaciers has its own hazards. Never paddle closer than about one quarter mile, even to a small glacier, as the waves from calving bergs can swamp your kayak (although in deep water these waves are generally smooth and rolling, and fairly easy to ride over bow first). If you land near a glacier to observe it or take pictures, draw your boats well above the waterline, as sudden waves can wash them off-shore. Also use care when camping to ensure that you and your boats are above the highest tide and wave line.

If you stay in Tierra del Fuego longer than, say, three hours, you're likely to experience a sudden change in weather, and these changes are the arbiters of paddling here. Sudden windstorms are the salient risk for kayakers; prevailing winds are southwesterly but can come from any direction. Rainfall is also high during the summer months, and the combination of wind and rain calls for the best tent you can afford. However, if you're well-equipped and well-trained, sporting about in these iceberg alleys is not just thrilling, but great fun. Some tabular bergy bits are big and flat enough to

land on (Picnic on an iceberg, anyone—no ants!), and there is always an infinity of shapes to watch as the larger bergs float slowly past.

GUIDES AND OUTFITTERS

Dynevor Expeditions in Chile runs a 12-day tour to Tierra del Fuego, by motor boat, horse, and kayak. Altue Sea Kayaking, also in Chile, offers trips farther north along the Pacific Coast.

DYNEVOR EXPEDITIONS
56-61-225-888
dynevor@entelchile.net
ALTUE SEA KAYAKING
56-2-232-1103
altue@entelchile.net
$220–$1,290 for 2–9 days

RECOMMENDED READING

■ *TREKKING IN THE PATAGONIAN ANDES,* Clem Lindenmayer (1998. $15.95. Lonely Planet.) Although oriented toward trekking, the information will be valuable to paddlers as well.
■ *VOYAGE OF THE BEAGLE,* Charles Darwin (1988. $1.95. Penguin Books.) A must-read. Darwin's brilliant observations and insights go far beyond biology.
■ *IN PATAGONIA,* Bruce Chatwin (1988. $13.95. Penguin Books.)

Lunch break at the head of Bahia Brookes, with guide Terry Brian (top) and a member of the group watching for calving icebergs (above). This close to a glacier, calving icebergs can cause dangerous waves.

Opposite: A glacier drops down to the sea from the Cordillera Alvear range, not far from Ushuaia, Argentina.

Isle of Mull

Match wits with the North Atlantic,
then embellish the tale over a pint or two.

There is no place on earth where nature has been more thoroughly groomed into civility than Great Britain. The overwhelming impression of the rural landscape here is that it has been carefully tended against the possibility that something—whether animal or plant—might stray beyond its assigned boundary. Fields and hills are green and cropped, bordered by neat stone walls and hedgerows; streams tumble obediently down well-defined courses; even the

forests appear trimmed and vaguely linear. It's a peaceful sort of feeling, like stepping into a James Herriot book, but there's little in the way of wilderness to tempt the adventurer.

That impression ends in a hissing crash of surf when you launch a kayak off the west coast of Scotland.

Against this shore, on the same latitude as Newfoundland, the North Atlantic Ocean expends the full force of its moods, checked only

Approaching Fingal's Cave on Staffa, a tiny island not far off the west coast of Mull and an excellent day trip.

NORTH
ATLANTIC

Outer Hebrides

Inner Hebrides

SKYE

RHUM
EIGG

TIREE

•Tobermory

ISLE OF
MULL   •Oban

SCOTLAND

• Glasgow

by the intermittent buffer of the 500-plus Hebridean Islands—which themselves channel the tides, waves, and winds of the ocean into furious currents, overfalls, and even whirlpools. It was unnerving, but exhilarating, to sit with my paddle held motionless and watch the walls of a narrow strait slide by at a jogging pace as a flooding tide swept me along, then to look ahead and see the entire surface of the sea drop a foot over some submerged obstacle, while just beyond, a directionless mass of waves churned and tumbled against each other. Traversing the west coast of Scotland earns you a master's degree in sea kayaking—but after each exam there's a pint of ale in a warm pub or the hospitable retreat of a farmhouse bed-and-breakfast often within walking distance of your launch site. Could life be better?

If the pubs, B&Bs, and scenery tempt you, but not the graduate school paddling, there's still plenty to do. The convoluted geography of the Hebridean Islands—the remains of their violent volcanic origins—results in thousands of sheltered lochs and bays which, when the wind is gentle, allow peaceful excursions to spot gray seals and nesting birds such as guillemots, kittiwakes,

and the clownish puffins popping in and out of their burrows. And on some fine summer days even the open Atlantic stills itself, so that with neap tides and a favorable long-range weather forecast more cautious (sane?) kayakers can hop from island to island over a deep blue, gently swelling sea.

The Hebrides comprise two main groups of islands. The Outer Hebrides, or Western Isles, include North and South Uist, and Harris and Lewis, which, confusingly, are actually only one island, the division being the result of clan feuding rather than geography. Scattered around the large islands is a myriad of smaller ones, many of them uninhabited and suitable for exploration and camping.

The Inner Hebrides form a ragged chain much closer to the mainland of Scotland— close enough, in fact, that the largest of them, Skye, can be reached via a bridge.

With reliable ferry service and well-developed towns, any of the big Hebridean islands makes a splendid base for kayak exploration, but the second-largest of the inner islands, Mull, is a particularly fine starting point for

---

AT A GLANCE

TRIP LENGTH 3–10 days
PADDLING DISTANCE 1–20 miles
PHYSICAL CHALLENGE ①②③④ 5
MENTAL CHALLENGE ①②③④ 5
PRIME TIME May–September

PRICE RANGE (INDEPENDENT TRIP) $360–$600 from Oban
PRICE RANGE (OUTFITTED GROUP TRIP) $1,500
STAGING CITY Tobermory, Scotland

Columnar basalt formations on Staffa; precise polygonal columns formed by the rapid cooling of lava.

both intermediate and advanced paddlers.

Mull can be reached by any one of three short ferry routes from the mainland. Thus, while you have the satisfaction of being on a real island (without the niggling stigma of a bridge), the travel time is short and the tariffs low. You can also paddle to Mull in good conditions if you wish; it's about a five-mile hop from the mainland town of Oban, itself just 90 miles northwest of Glasgow. The Sound of Mull, the channel between the island and the mainland, is sheltered from the open sea, though still subject to tidal currents.

Despite its proximity to the mainland, Mull is relatively unpopulated, with most of its 3,000 residents living in villages along the 300-plus miles of coastline. This population figure actually represents something of a rebound from the drastically low numbers after the Highland Clearances ended in the 19th century; previously the population ranged upwards of 10,000. The interior of the island, especially the southern region, is mountainous, the high point reaching over 3,000 feet at Ben More.

At the north end of Mull is possibly the most beautiful port in Scotland, Tobermory, with striking multicolored waterfront buildings lending the whole town an unquenchably cheerful air, even when Atlantic storms cover it in dense gray mist. From Tobermory a road system circles the island, offering access to several lochs which, depending on weather and wind direction, offer sheltered paddling for "messing about." You can also explore the Sound of Mull between Tobermory and Craignure. Just east of Craignure is the

Opposite: Old stone crofter's cottages like this one are disappearing or being turned into weekend homes.

Good landing beach on the Isle of Rhum, midway between Mull and the Isle of Skye, to the north.

magnificent 13th-century Duart Castle, which is open to visitors (if the castle looks familiar, you might have seen it as Sean Connery's, uh, "house," in the movie *Entrapment*).

Experienced open-water paddlers can fully exploit Mull's potential by heading offshore, especially to the beautiful Threshnish Isles, a string of tiny volcanic nubbins extending out from the west coast like bits of foam flung off a wave crest. Castle ruins and seabird colonies make for exciting exploration, while fairly short crossings (2 miles or less) allow fast retreats if the wind kicks up. And east of the Threshnish Isles is the stunning island of Staffa and its polygonal basalt columns and booming sea caves. Taking in these islands during a circumnavigation of Mull would make a trip to be relived for years.

While Mull could pass as the quintessen-tial Hebridean island, with over 500 more to choose from, it is obviously just a beginning. Wherever you go, don't forget the most vital rule for paddling here:

Get back before the pub closes.

SUGGESTED ROUTES

Paddling distances in the Mull area can be any-where from a mile or two exploring a loch to about 20 miles for an exploration of the Threshnish Isles and Staffa. The physical and mental challenge ratings range from 1 if you stay in the harbor or lochs, to a solid 4 if you attempt open crossings or a circumnavigation.

The best single- or multi-day paddle off Mull, for those with excellent open-water skills, is to the Threshnish Isles and Staffa. In good weather—not by any means a daily occurrence it's an easy paddle from the sandy shores of Calgary Bay (a 10-mile drive from Tobermory, with camping and toilets) to the Threshnish chain, no island being more than two miles from the next. The first sizeable island, Cairn na Burgh Beg, boasts the remains of two 18th-century castles, impressive for their location rather than condition or splendor. There are good, sandy landing sites and primitive camping spots (unnofficial, so no reservations are needed or possible) on Lunga, the long middle island, although you'll be sharing it with multiple thousands of raucous auks and puffins. From Lunga there's a clear view of the last island in the chain, the well-named Dutchman's Cap.

Five miles east of the Dutchman's Cap, breaking the ocean swells in solitude (except for the tourist boats that visit it daily), is the island of Staffa, the southern face of which boasts one of the most surreal formations on earth: a bastion of tightly packed basalt columns cracked into precise polygonal shapes by the cooling of the volcanic matrix that formed the core of the island. The name Staffa derives from the Nordic word for pillars, bestowed when the Vikings commanded these coasts.

Awe-inspiring though the pillars may be, the caves worn into them by the pounding sea are even more so. The most famous, Fingal's Cave, echoes with a mighty booming roar with each wave that surges through its entrance. The sound inspired Felix Mendelssohn to compose his *Die Fingalshölle* after a visit in 1829. More recently the writer Ian Anderson, in the book *Across Hebridean Seas,* wrote "There is the deep cave music of the sea, when one feels that the beating of its waves in the depths of a solitary cavern echoes the deep notes of the great

THE PLAID TRUTH ABOUT TARTANS

Everyone knows that Scottish clans have been identified by their distinctive tartan patterns for centuries. Everyone, however, is wrong. The idea of a unique tartan as a clan totem did not become popular until well into the 19th century.

The tartan began as a rough, homespun length of cloth imbued with muted earth-tone colors that made it effective camouflage against the highland heather. It was worn wrapped around the waist and thrown over the shoulder. Not until it was adopted as a sign of unity among the Jacobites in the early 18th century did the tartan begin to make a political statement. A ban on the wearing of tartans was instated in 1747, and subsequently lifted in 1782. After Sir Walter Scott wrote his thrilling accounts of the clans, the few existing genuine clan patterns became models for the invention of countless others. Still, it's fun for those of Scottish ancestry to find their own tartan pattern among the hundreds now offered in every shop near the main tourist routes.

Top: Mull on the horizon viewed from the west coast of the mainland. Above: The colorful harbor of Tobermory at the north end of Mull.

by a scant 100-yard-wide channel.

If you decide to attempt a circumnavigation of Mull, there are also well-spaced camping spots at Loch Scridain, Loch Na Keal, Loch Spelve, and Craignure.

Mull serves nicely as a base for more adventurous kayaking expeditions as well. To the west are the islands of Coll and Tiree, a 7-mile crossing at the nearest points (fortunately, tidal currents are not much of an issue here). At Arinagour on Coll you can rent mountain bikes to explore the short network of roads, or paddle around to the wildlife refuge on the southeast corner of the island. Looking toward the sunset from the west coast of Coll, there's nothing but Atlantic between you and Canada.

If you find mere open-ocean crossings a bit tedious, you might want to challenge what many consider the single most advanced sea kayak route in the world: the Gulf of Corryvreckan, a channel between the islands of Jura and Scarba, about 15 miles south of Mull. On a spring flood tide, the current running west through Corryvreckan hits 8 knots, while an eddy current running the opposite direction can also hit 8 knots. The juncture of the two currents produces savage waves and vortices, while in one spot a submerged reef called *Camas nam Bairneach* sucks the surface of the sea into a vast whirlpool known as the Hag. In addition, the seabed under the strait drops several hundred feet, causing numerous overfalls. Running the bare mile length of Corryvreckan requires not only absolute mastery of the boat, but precise timing and intimate knowledge of the chaotic currents. Even if you are an expert paddler with a bombproof roll, Corryvreckan should only be attempted in the company of an experienced local paddler. Contact one of the many local sea kayaking clubs for information.

WHAT TO EXPECT

This is a civilized country bordering an uncivilized ocean. Traveling in Scotland is a delight,

pipes of a mighty cathedral organ." A fitting bit of imagery, especially in light of the pipelike columns that surround the chambers. Braver kayakers than I have paddled right into Fingal's Cave and the even larger McKinnon's Cave.

From Staffa it's about four miles northeast to the shelter of Ulva (another Norse derivation, this from "Wolf Island," an intriguing name given that there were wolves in Scotland until the 18th century; were they on the islands too?). Camping is allowed on Ulva with permission from the owners. Ulva is separated from the "mainland" of Mull

Lunga, the middle island of the Threshnish Isles, offers good "unofficial" primitive camping sites.

thanks to what are likely the friendliest natives on earth. If you can't get what you ask for here, *you're* doing something wrong.

Obviously, in such a highly developed country provisioning isn't a problem. You can obtain most groceries you need in Tobermory on Mull (there's also a deli and even a distillery there), but for major stocking up it's better to use Oban or Glasgow.

The best resource for information on paddling equipment, local rentals, and regional clubs (a strong presence in Great Britain) is the British Canoe Union. Their website can be found at www.bcu.org.uk.

Although Mull is increasing in popularity among U.K. paddlers, it's still by no means

A sandy landing site along the sheltered Ross of Mull on the south coast of the island.

overrun. Land-based tourism, however, hits a peak during summer, when you might have difficulty planning an inn-to-inn tour without reservations. Consider going in September, when tourists thin out considerably yet the weather remains mostly splendid.

The best way to find accommodations in and near Tobermory is to ask at the tourist office (open April through September). They have listings of several lovely bed-and-breakfast establishments scattered throughout the island.

There are several semi-organized government campgrounds along the coast of Mull, with basic facilities such as restrooms or outhouses. On deserted beaches you may camp where you like; if any habitation is within view you should ask permission (which is very rarely refused). Private campgrounds have more amenities, but are mostly located along roads rather than on beaches.

Even if you skip Corryvreckan, paddling in Scotland requires planning, excellent paddling skills, and proper clothing. Long-range weather reports are your best friend here. They can be obtained over the radio, or by calling the local coast guard station (there is one in Oban). You'll also need tidal charts, obtained at marine supply stores in the area you're visiting. Use caution, however—local variations in timing and current

PUFFINS

The most unmistakable bird in Scotland is the puffin, with its clownlike face, huge, candy-striped bill, and wings that seem too ridiculously short to get the bird airborne—only furious flapping keeps them aloft. Puffins nest in large colonies on islands and promontories, excavating tunnels into soft turf that are as deep as six feet, where the females lay a single white egg. The adults bring home small fish, often lining up five or six in a row in the beak in an improbable display of dexterity.

Those tiny wings work better underwater, where the puffin does its hunting. They have been known to dive to over 150 feet, but generally stay within 50 feet of the surface, in pursuit of herring, capelin, and small cod.

might not match the chart. And always remember that weather conditions can change much faster than weather reports do. I carry a handheld barometer to help keep track of local trends.

The Gulf Stream ensures that sea temperatures off Scotland are not as cold as they might otherwise be at this latitude, but the water is still in the 50s (F), and adequate clothing is essential for safe paddling. For strictly coastal paddling you should be fine with a full thermal stretch inner layer and a rainproof shell, but for any off-shore excursions neoprene provides a better buffer, and a dry suit wouldn't be overkill.

Fog and rain are common, so a deck-mounted compass, and the knowledge to use it properly, is a vital piece of kit. Take careful visual bearings before launching on crossings, and calculate the effects of cross currents in advance.

GUIDES AND OUTFITTERS

Maine Island Kayaks, in conjunction with Anglesey Sea and Surf Center in Wales, runs a tour of several Scottish islands, usually including Mull, from a 110-foot ship that serves as a floating base. It includes full B&B accommodations with all meals and equipment. The tour stops at several distilleries for demonstrations of traditional Scottish methods to combat hypothermia.

MAINE ISLAND KAYAKS

70 Luther St.
Peaks Island, ME 04108
800-796-2373
www.maineisland.kayak.com
$1,500 for 10 days

RECOMMENDED READING

- *MULL AND IONA,* P.A. MacNab (2000. $9.95. Luath Press.) Very good, detailed information about Mull.
- *SCOTTISH ISLAND HOPPING,* Hubert Andrews (1997. $17.00. Polygon Press.) A thorough, but more broad-based guide to the Scottish islands.

The Orkney & Shetland Islands

Explore a land where seafaring has defined its people.

Step ashore on the windswept coast of Scotland's Orkney or Shetland Islands and you'll notice what at first seem to be but subtle signs of their Scandinavian past: place names, the longship-like lines of a Ness Yole rowing craft, the lilting accent of shopkeepers and hotel clerks. But if you happen to stumble into the Shetland town of Lerwick during the January *Up Helly Aa* festival, when hordes of torchbearing revelers in horned helmets drag a

longship through the streets and then set it afire in classic chieftain funeral fashion, you'll be left with no doubt that the Viking spirit still burns fiercely in the hearts of the residents.

The story behind the islands' intertwined culture goes back over 1,000 years. By the early ninth century the Vikings were already becoming jaded with their summer pillaging runs to Britain and mainland Europe, and were looking for places to settle permanently (they were,

The Isle of Hoy, one of the southernmost of the Orkney Islands.

SHETLAND
ISLANDS
MAINLAND
● Lerwick

ORKNEY
ISLANDS   ⌐FAIR ISLE

● Kirkwall
MAINLAND

NORTH
ATLANTIC

● John O'Groats

Outer Hebrides

Inner Hebrides

SCOTLAND

after all, farmers at heart). Thus began a very different sort of invasion, one with a peaceful end, for no sooner had the Vikings carved out territory in lands they had formerly terrorized, than they began to revert to the agrarian ways of their ancestors. Within a century or two the Vikings were completely integrated into their adopted communities, and they had even introduced customs that were to have long-lasting effects in their new home—for example, a form of government we now know as parliamentary democracy.

But while the ghosts of the Vikings and their sleek longships provide perhaps the most stirring backdrop, the story of the farmers and herders who first colonized Orkney and Shetland is much, much older. Houses and tombs dating back to the fourth millennium B.C. are scattered about in astonishing quantity; in fact, Orkney has a greater density of prehistoric sites—over a thousand—than anyplace in Europe. A primary explanation for this is that trees have always been scarce here, thus virtually all building on the islands was done with stone, which stood a greater chance of surviving eons of North Atlantic weathering. The best-known archaeological site on the main island of Orkney, Skara Brae, was completely unknown until 1850, when a winter gale uncovered it, perfectly preserved after being buried for some 4,500 years. Even stone beds and tables were still in place.

It's fitting that these two groups of islands—170 in all, only 30-odd of which are inhabited—should share the culture of two great seafaring peoples. Everywhere in both Orkney and Shetland the tang of salt air is a constant sweetness on the palate, and rarely are you even out of sight of the ocean—nowhere in Shetland is it more than three miles away, nor in Orkney more than four. Always you're aware of the mighty presence of the North Atlantic; the land itself seems to exist solely for the purpose of providing a coast. And kayaking those coasts is, more than anywhere else in the U.K., a trip into history.

AT A GLANCE

TRIP LENGTH 3–10 days
PADDLING DISTANCE Highly variable
PHYSICAL CHALLENGE 1 2 ③ ④ 5
MENTAL CHALLENGE 1 2 3 ④ 5
PRIME TIME May–August

PRICE RANGE (INDEPENDENT TRIP) $550–$900 from John O'Groats or Aberdeen
PRICE RANGE (OUTFITTED GROUP TRIP) $1,200
STAGING CITY Kirkwall in Orkney; Lerwick in Shetland, Scotland

Consider the paddle to the small island of Mousa, which rises from the sea like a two-humped green camel only a mile off the southeast coast of Mainland Shetland (the largest islands of both the Shetland and Orkney chains are called, confusingly, Mainland). As you head out across the bouncy gray channel from Leebitton, the small dorsal fins of harbor porpoises flash here and there as they feed on small fish, and a gray or common seal might pop its head up to inspect you. But soon your attention is drawn to something else: a massive stone tower toward the south end of Mousa, slightly conical in shape, standing over 40 feet tall. It's called Mousa Broch, a defensive structure built during a period of invasion and resistance in the Iron Age, sometime around 400 B.C. One of many brochs scattered throughout the islands, Mousa's is one of the few still intact (most were

raided for their stone). After landing in the bay north of the broch, near where a small tourist ferry docks, you can enter the tower through the seaward door and climb the stairway sandwiched between the inner and outer walls, just as its defenders would have done carrying bows and spears 2,000 years ago. The view from the parapet makes it clear that the broch's designed height was no accident: You can see clean over the lower parts of the island to the eastern sea approaches, an obvious tactical advantage. (Ironically, archaeologists are unsure who built the brochs—the island's inhabitants or the invaders.) You complete the tour of Mousa on a trail that winds past seal colonies and tern nesting grounds, before heading back to Leebitton.

This short-excursion approach to, what shall we call it, archeo-kayaking, is one of the

Opposite: Foula, the westernmost of the Shetland Islands, lies some 15 miles off the west coast of Mainland.
Above: Approaching a sea cave entrance, Shapensay Island, Orkneys.

SELKIES

As you paddle along rocky shores in Orkney and Shetland, you'll see many seals, mostly gray and common seals, sunning themselves on rocks or cavorting offshore. Look closely at them, especially into those soulful brown eyes, for some might not be seals at all.

For centuries, fishermen in Orkney and Shetland—as well as County Donegal in Ireland—have told tales of selkies (called the Roane in Ireland). A female selkie can discard her seal-like skin and travel on land as a lovely maiden. If a man discovers this

skin and hides it, she will become his wife—dutiful, loyal, and talented, but always wistful for the sea. She might bear the man beautiful children, and be a loving mother, but if she ever finds her seal skin, she will abandon her family and return to the sea.

And what of male selkies? Unfortunately for human women, they don't come ashore as handsome men. Instead they can call forth storms and even overturn boats, to extract revenge when fishermen kill seals.

best ways to experience the many islands of Shetland and Orkney. Most trips—and there are dozens of possibilities from solitary brochs to excavated villages—can be done in a day or even a half day, and are thus easier to slot into weather windows between the more boisterous moods of the North Atlantic Ocean. Since even the main islands are small, if the wind is blowing onshore at your first choice of routes, you can just drive to the other side and launch in an offshore breeze. Last, but not least, day trips mean there's a pint and maybe even a warm bed waiting at journey's end. You can base out of either capital (Kirkwall on Orkney; Lerwick on Shetland), and find innumerable short paddles within a 10-mile drive if you have a car, or indeed without driving at all, simply heading out of the harbor, although the latter puts you at the mercy of local conditions. Nevertheless, this is Scottish-style sea kayaking at its best: Challenge the sea by day; relax in the pub by night.

Orkney, and (50 miles farther north) Shetland even more so, are at the remote end of the British Isles, and getting to them takes a bit of planning. But the rewards are certainly worth it, in landscape, wildlife, history, and people.

Oh yes, the people. Think of the average, outgoing Scot, with just a little extra burly self-sufficiency, and a slight Scandinavian drollness to the humor. Consider the grizzled fisherman overlooking the notorious Pentland Firth between Orkney and Scotland, revealing, deadpan, the thrifty Scottish cure for seasickness: "It's simple, lad, we just lean over the rail with a five-pound note between our teeth."

LONGSHIP DESCENDANTS

Men will quake with terror
Ere the seventy sea-oars
Gain their well-earned respite
From the labors of the ocean.
Norwegian arms are driving
This iron-studded dragon
Down the storm-tossed river
Like an eagle with wings beating
—Snorri Sturluson: *King Harald's Saga*

The Viking longship is possibly the most recognized historic sailing ship in the world. Its unmistakable sleek lines, the dragon-head prow, the round shield at each rowing station, and the big, square sail, present an image so ingrained as to be iconic.

The longship was, in its time, the finest seafaring warship ever designed: It was fast (modern replicas have exceeded 10 knots under sail) and could be rowed when the wind died or more maneuverability was needed. A shallow draft let it range up rivers and into estuaries, yet it was seaworthy enough to explore the reaches of the North Atlantic Ocean. Accommodations were, shall we say, suited to the Vikings' burly image: a tent on the open deck, which might on long voyages shelter both men and stock animals.

The longships' time is past, but you'll see obvious evidence of their influence in the harbors of Orkney and Shetland, mainly in smaller craft designed for fishing. The lapstrake construction (called clinker in Europe), with its overlapping hull planks, is one prevalent feature, along with a grace of line that's difficult to measure objectively. These boats, although not designed for crossing oceans, are nevertheless superbly seaworthy for their tasks (very much like another type of small craft we know). One particularly beautiful rowing craft is called a Ness Yole; the design is very common in Shetland.

Approaching a tidal pour-over near Hillswick on the west coast of Mainland, Shetland Islands.

SUGGESTED ROUTES

You'll want large-scale OS charts for route planning, as long stretches of unapproachable shore alternate with sand beaches and sheltered fjords. There is considerably more vertical coastline in Shetland than in Orkney.

SHETLAND

Mousa and its broch are just a mile off the group of villages known as Sandwick, about eight miles south of Lerwick. A ferry goes to Mousa from Leebitton if conditions are too rough for paddling. Other intriguing sites to

consider in Shetland include the remains of the 12th-century church on St. Ninian's Isle (which is actually connected to Mainland by a narrow strip of sand called a tombolo). For something different, paddle out to the sea caves, arches, and stacks of Papa Stour, an island just off the west coast of Shetland.

One area to avoid on Shetland is Sullom Voe (it evens sounds like someplace to avoid, doesn't it?), a long inlet on the north end of Mainland. There is an enormous oil and gas terminal there, just north of the town of Brae, with heavy tanker traffic.

Ancient stone carvings like this one are found throughout the islands of western and northern Scotland, reminders of the earlier inhabitants of these isolated lands.

ORKNEY

In Orkney, consider paddling to the Broch of Gurness (on the rough Eynhallow Sound; use caution) and Skara Brae (on the exposed west coast). In addition, there are dozens of lesser-known sites to be discovered simply by landing and looking around on likely promontories—you'll find that the human taste in sea views has changed little in two millennia.

WHAT TO EXPECT

Although remote—or perhaps because of it—the capitals of both Orkney and Shetland are

well equipped with hotels and basic services such as groceries and laundromats.

Kirkwall, in Orkney, is a rather sprawling town saved by a single feature: the lovely 12th-century St. Magnus cathedral. Despite erosion of the sandstone it's still an awe-inspiring presence. Good hotels include the centrally located Albert, and the more interesting Ayre, on the waterfront.

Lerwick, Shetland's capital, has more options in guest houses than Kirkwall, such as the Alder Lodge and the Glen Orchy House. For cheap stays, try making reservations in a *Böd* (pronounced sort of like *bird*), one of a series of small, very basic cottages or huts available for rent by the night. You can find out about them at the Lerwick tourist office.

Make sure you have all your paddling gear with you (there's no problem taking hardshell kayaks on the ferries). If you get a chance for a side trip, take the ferry to Fair Isle, a nubbin in the ocean about halfway between Orkney and Shetland. You can buy a sweater there that will repel water almost as well as a Gore-Tex parka.

If you crave more solitude, or are on a tight budget, primitive camping is generally allowed anywhere along the coast in Orkney and Shetland, although you are expected to ask permission if you're within sight of a farm. Camping does allow you to explore more remote stretches of the coast, which will get you closer to the wildlife of the islands, especially their birds, which nest in thousands on Orkney and millions on the cliffs of Shetland. Puffins, fulmars, gannets, and razorbills are attracted to these precipitous surroundings; on gentler shores, where coastal heather crowds the high tide line, you'll see skuas, plovers, and other waders, and handsome eider ducks. And of course the final advantage to a week out in the rough is that the pint of best bitter at the end tastes just that much better.

Much the same paddling cautions apply for

Gannett colony, Isle of Ness. These islands are subject to the worst weather the North Atlantic and the North Sea can throw at them; sunny, calm days are pleasant rarities.

Orkney and Shetland as for mainland Scotland's west coast—if anything, more so. The islands are subject to the worst weather the northern Atlantic can muster, and warm sun and calm water are always to be considered transient conditions. But those glorious windows are well worth waiting for. Tidal currents, as a rule, are not as hazardous here as off the mainland of Scotland, but they are still a factor in the channels between the islands, where opposing wind and current quickly creates dangerous chop.

There still aren't many sea kayakers in the islands, and most of those are from Great Britain. So you'll be something of a novelty—always good for conversation and advice.

Guides and Outfitters

Maine Island Kayaks runs summer trips to Orkney, using a comfortable 110-foot ship as a base for day paddles. The trips depart from Anglesey, in Wales, and last about 12 days. They are recommended for experienced paddlers. Call for pricing.

MAINE ISLAND KAYAKS

70 Luther St.
Peaks Island, ME 04108
800-796-2373
www.maineislandkayak.com

Recommended Reading

- *SCOTLAND, THE ROUGH GUIDE,* Dave Abram et al (1996. $16.95. The Rough Guides.) Good information about out-of-the-way destinations.
- *KIDNAPPED,* Robert Louis Stevenson (preferably the edition illustrated by N.C. Wyeth). (1913. $24.95. Charles Scribner's Sons.) The classic tale of adventure on the Scottish coast.

PHOTO CREDITS

José Azel / Aurora: 6, 11, 162 (right), 172 (top), 177, 181 (bottom)

Peter Barker / Panos Pictures: 70 (bottom)

Fred Bavendam / Minden Pictures: 161

Matthew Benson / Tony Stone Images: 158

Andrea Booher / Tony Stone Images: 56 (bottom)

Per Breiehagen: 9, 18-19, 20 (right), 42 (both), 44, 45, 46, 48(both)

Dugald Bremner: 131 (top)

Skip Brown: 106 (left), 108 (bottom), 116, 117

Mike Caldwell / Tony Stone Images: 194

Paul Chesley / Tony Stone Images: 21 (right), 96 (top), 102

Richard Cooke / Tony Stone Images: 96 (bottom)

Neil Cooper/ Panos Pictures: 85

Neil Cranston: 163 (center), 196, 163 (center), 205

Chad Ehlers / Tony Stone Images: 139

Thomas Ernsting / Aurora: 101

Dave Etheridge / Nantahala Outdoor Center: 40

Kelly Fischer / Nantahala Outdoor Center: 32 (bottom)

Bruce Forster / Tony Stone Images: 62

Nigel Foster: 192 (bottom), 199, 200, 207, 208, 209

Alain le Garsmeur / Panos Pictures: 76 (bottom)

Henry Georgi: 8, 20 (left), 24-25

Brian Goddard / Panos Pictures: 77

D. Goering: 78 (both), 81, 83, 84 (top)

Malcolm Gunn: 184, 186-187

Jonathan Hanson: 106 (right), 126 (both), 132, 133, 162 (left), 164 (both), 166, 167, 168

Blaine Harrington: 144 (both), 149, 159

Bill Hatcher: 50 (top), 56 (top), 134

Michael N. Heiko / Bruce Coleman Inc.: 47

John Higginson / Tony Stone Images: 192 (top), 198 (top)

Johanna Huber / SIME: 60 (top), 107 (left), 154 (both), 157, 160

Alison Hughes: 118 (both), 120, 122, 123

David Job / Tony Stone Images: 34

Roderick Johnson / Panos Pictures: 124

Kayak Africa: 21 (center), 70 (top), 72, 73, 74, 76 (top), 80, 82

David McLain / Aurora: 110-111, 112, 115

Joseph McNally / Image Bank: 30

Gabe Palacio / Aurora: 130

Douglas Peebles: 99

Michael Powers: 16, 86 (bottom), 89, 90, 91 (top), 107 (center), 136 (bottom), 138, 141, 142, 143 (both), 153 (bottom), 182 (both), 189, 191 (both)

Donovan Reese: 198 (bottom)

Joel Rogers: 2-3, 22 (bottom), 26, 27, 29, 50 (bottom), 57, 63, 66 (both), 67, 68, 69 (both), 104, 105, 113, 114, 131 (bottom), 152-153 (top), 156

Galen Rowell: 13, 32 (top), 36-37, 41, 86 (top), 92-93, 94, 128-129, 163 (left), 190

David Sanger: 58 (bottom), 98

Dominic Sansoni / Panos Pictures: 125

Kevin Schafer: 52-53, 58 (top), 60 (bottom), 150, 174-175, 176, 195, 201, 202 (bottom), 204

Eugene G. Schulz: 84 (bottom)

Giovanni Simeone / SIME: 21 (left), 54, 55, 58 (center), 64-65, 197

Scott Spiker: 10, 12, 22 (top), 28, 88, 91 (bottom), 95, 103, 148 (bottom)

Hans Strand / Tony Stone Images: 136 (top)

Ralph Talmont / Aurora: 107 (right), 147

Darryl Torckler / Tony Stone Images: 146

John Turk: 169, 170, 172 (bottom), 179, 181 (top)

Paul Wakefield / Tony Stone Images: 202 (top)

Stuart Westmorland / Tony Stone Images: 100

Konrad Wothe / Minden Pictures: 148 (top)

George Wuerthner: 38, 39, 108 (top)

INDEX